I0762544

MEDITERRANEAN
FLAVORS

Publications International, Ltd.

Copyright © 2026 Publications International, Ltd.
All rights reserved. This publication may not be reproduced or quoted in whole or in part by any means whatsoever without written permission from:

Louis Weber, CEO
Publications International, Ltd.
5250 Old Orchard Road, Suite 500
Skokie, IL 60077

Permission is never granted for commercial purposes.

Art on front cover and throughout copyright © Shutterstock.com.

Pictured on the back cover *(left to right):* Sheet Pan Mediterranean Chicken *(page 134)*, Pasta all'Arrabbiata *(page 79)* and Mediterranean Salad *(page 27)*.

ISBN: 979-8-89746-143-1

Manufactured in China.

8 7 6 5 4 3 2 1

Microwave Cooking: Microwave ovens vary in wattage. Use the cooking times as guidelines and check for doneness before adding more time.

WARNING: Food preparation, baking and cooking involve inherent dangers: misuse of electric products, sharp electric tools, boiling water, hot stoves, allergic reactions, foodborne illnesses and the like, pose numerous potential risks. Publications International, Ltd. (PIL) assumes no responsibility or liability for any damages you may experience as a result of following recipes, instructions, tips or advice in this publication.

While we hope this publication helps you find new ways to eat delicious foods, you may not always achieve the results desired due to variations in ingredients, cooking temperatures, typos, errors, omissions or individual cooking abilities.

Let's get social!

 @Publications_International

 @PublicationsInternational

www.pilbooks.com

CONTENTS

JALAPEÑO FETA DIP

MAKES ABOUT 1 CUP

- **1 jalapeño pepper, halved, stemmed and seeded**
- **½ red onion, halved and separated**
- **3 tablespoons plus 1 teaspoon extra virgin olive oil, divided**
- **8 ounces feta cheese**
- **1 tablespoon water**
- **Crostini (recipe follows) and/or cut-up fresh vegetables**

1 Preheat oven to 400°F. Place jalapeño and onion on small baking sheet; drizzle with 1 teaspoon oil and stir to coat. Arrange vegetables cut sides down on baking sheet. Bake 20 minutes or until vegetables are softened and slightly charred around edges. Let stand until cool enough to handle.

2 Scrape skin from jalapeño with paring knife. Coarsely chop jalapeño and onion.

3 Combine feta, remaining 3 tablespoons oil and water in food processor; process until smooth and fluffy. Add vegetables; pulse 6 to 8 times or until blended but still chunky. Serve with crostini. Store dip in airtight container in refrigerator up to 1 week.

CROSTINI

Slice one loaf of French bread about ¼ inch thick into desired number of slices. Brush both sides with olive oil and lightly season with salt and pepper, if desired. Place on baking sheet. Broil 2 minutes per side or until toasted. Crostini can also be grilled. Place directly on grate and grill until toasted on both sides.

SOUTHERN ITALIAN EGGPLANT DIP

MAKES 6 TO 8 SERVINGS

- **1 large eggplant (about 1¾ pounds), peeled and cut into 1-inch cubes**
- **3 tablespoons extra virgin olive oil, divided**
- **¾ teaspoon salt, divided**
- **1 can (about 14 ounces) diced tomatoes, drained**
- **¼ cup chopped red onion**
- **2 tablespoons capers, rinsed and drained**
- **2 tablespoons red wine vinegar**
- **1 clove garlic, minced**
- **1 teaspoon honey**
- **¼ cup chopped fresh parsley**
- **Black pepper**
- **Shredded Parmesan cheese (optional)**
- **Assorted crackers or Crostini (page 5)**

1 Preheat oven to 375°F. Line baking sheet with parchment paper. Place eggplant on baking sheet. Drizzle with 1 tablespoon oil and sprinkle with ½ teaspoon salt; toss to coat. Spread eggplant in single layer.

2 Bake 35 to 40 minutes or until tender, stirring after 20 minutes.

3 Combine tomatoes, onion, capers, vinegar, garlic, honey, remaining 2 tablespoons oil and ¼ teaspoon salt in large bowl; mix well. Stir in eggplant. Gently stir in parsley; season with additional salt and pepper.

4 Cool to room temperature or refrigerate until ready to serve. Garnish with cheese; serve with crackers or crostini.

BRUSCHETTA

MAKES 8 SERVINGS (1 CUP TOPPING)

- 4 plum tomatoes, seeded and diced
- ½ cup packed fresh basil leaves, finely chopped
- 5 tablespoons extra virgin olive oil, divided
- 2 cloves garlic, minced
- 2 teaspoons finely chopped oil-packed sun-dried tomatoes
- ¼ teaspoon salt
- ⅛ teaspoon black pepper
- 16 slices Italian bread
- 2 tablespoons grated Parmesan cheese

1 Combine fresh tomatoes, basil, 3 tablespoons oil, garlic, sun-dried tomatoes, salt and pepper in large bowl; mix well. Let stand at room temperature 1 hour to allow flavors to blend.

2 Preheat oven to 375°F. Place bread on medium baking sheet. Brush remaining 2 tablespoons oil over one side of bread slices; sprinkle with cheese. Bake 6 to 8 minutes or until toasted.

3 Top each bread slice with 1 tablespoon tomato mixture.

BASIL CANNELLINI DIP

MAKES ABOUT 1½ CUPS

- 1 can (about 15 ounces) cannellini or Great Northern beans
- 1 clove garlic
- 2 tablespoons extra virgin olive oil
- 3 tablespoons chopped fresh basil
- 2 tablespoons fresh lemon juice
- Salt and black pepper
- Crostini (page 5) and/or cut-up vegetables

1 Drain beans, reserving ¼ cup liquid. Rinse and drain beans.

2 With motor running, drop garlic clove through feed tube of food processor; process until finely chopped. Add beans, reserved liquid and oil; process until smooth.

3 Stir in basil. Season to taste with salt and pepper. Spread on crostini to serve.

ROASTED EGGPLANT SPREAD ▸

MAKES 10 SERVINGS

- 1 eggplant (1 pound)
- 1 medium tomato
- 1 tablespoon fresh lemon juice
- 1 tablespoon chopped fresh basil *or* 1 teaspoon dried basil
- 2 teaspoons chopped fresh thyme *or* ¾ teaspoon dried thyme
- 1 clove garlic, minced
- ¼ teaspoon salt
- 1 tablespoon extra virgin olive oil
- Focaccia (page 166) or Crostini (page 5)

1 Preheat oven to 400°F. Pierce eggplant with fork in several places. Place on oven rack; roast 10 minutes.

2 Cut off stem from tomato; place in small baking pan. Bake eggplant and tomato 40 minutes. Let vegetables stand until cool enough to handle. Peel vegetables; coarsely chop eggplant.

3 Combine, eggplant, tomato, lemon juice, basil, thyme, garlic and salt in food processor; process until chunky. With motor running, slowly add oil and process until well blended. Refrigerate 3 hours or overnight. Serve with focaccia.

GOAT CHEESE-STUFFED FIGS

MAKES 7 SERVINGS

- 7 fresh firm ripe figs
- 7 slices prosciutto
- 1 package (4 ounces) goat cheese
- Black pepper

1 Preheat broiler. Line baking sheet with foil. Cut figs in half vertically. Cut prosciutto slices in half lengthwise to create 14 pieces (about 4 inches long and 1 inch wide).

2 Spread 1 teaspoon goat cheese onto cut side of each fig half. Wrap prosciutto slice around fig and goat cheese. Sprinkle with pepper.

3 Broil about 4 minutes or until cheese softens and figs are heated through.

MEDITERRANEAN-INSPIRED DEVILED EGGS ▸

MAKES 12 APPETIZERS

- **¼ cup finely diced cucumber**
- **¼ cup finely diced tomato**
- **2 teaspoons fresh lemon juice**
- **⅛ teaspoon salt**
- **6 hard-cooked eggs, peeled and sliced in half lengthwise**
- **⅓ cup roasted garlic or any flavor hummus**
- **Chopped fresh parsley (optional)**

1 Combine cucumber, tomato, lemon juice and salt in small bowl; gently mix.

2 Remove yolks from eggs; discard. Spoon 1 heaping teaspoon hummus into each egg half. Top with ½ teaspoon cucumber-tomato mixture and parsley, if desired. Serve immediately.

ZESTY TOMATO BRUSCHETTA

MAKES 2 CUPS (18 SERVINGS)

- **¼ cup red wine vinegar**
- **1 clove garlic, minced**
- **½ teaspoon salt**
- **½ teaspoon Italian seasoning**
- **½ teaspoon Dijon mustard**
- **1 teaspoon sugar**
- **Black pepper**
- **¼ cup extra virgin olive oil**
- **3 medium tomatoes, seeded and finely chopped**
- **¼ cup finely chopped red onion**
- **1 tablespoon chopped fresh basil**
- **1 loaf Italian or French bread**

1 Whisk vinegar, garlic, salt, Italian seasoning, mustard and sugar in medium bowl; season with pepper. Whisk in oil in thin steady stream until well blended. Combine 2 tablespoons vinaigrette, tomatoes, onion and basil in another medium bowl.

2 Slice bread into 18 thin slices. Whisk vinaigrette again to blend, if necessary; brush all over one side of each bread slice. Grill or broil bread until golden, turning once. Top toast with tomato mixture; serve immediately.

NOTE

Tomato mixture and toast can be made ahead; store separately and assemble just before serving.

SPINACH FETA TRIANGLES

MAKES 5 DOZEN APPETIZERS

- ¼ cup extra virgin olive oil
- ½ cup chopped onion
- 2 eggs
- 3 packages (10 ounces each) frozen chopped spinach, thawed and squeezed dry
- 16 ounces feta cheese, drained and crumbled
- ½ cup minced fresh parsley
- 2 tablespoons chopped fresh oregano *or* 1 teaspoon dried oregano
- Salt and black pepper
- 1 package (16 ounces) frozen phyllo dough, thawed
- 1 cup (2 sticks) butter, melted

1. Preheat oven to 375°F. Heat oil in small skillet over medium-high heat. Add onion; cook and stir 5 to 7 minutes until golden brown. Remove from heat; let cool 10 minutes.
2. Beat eggs in large bowl. Stir in onion, spinach, cheese, parsley and oregano; season with salt and pepper.
3. Unroll phyllo on large sheet of waxed paper. Fold phyllo crosswise into thirds. Use scissors to cut along folds into thirds. Cover phyllo with plastic wrap and damp, clean kitchen towel.*
4. Lay one strip of phyllo at a time on flat surface and brush with melted butter. Fold strip in half lengthwise. Brush with butter. Place rounded teaspoonful of spinach filling on one end of strip; fold over one corner to make triangle. Continue folding end to end, keeping edges straight. Brush top with butter. Repeat with remaining phyllo and filling until all filling is used up.
5. Place triangles in single layer on ungreased baking sheet, seam side down. Bake 20 minutes or until lightly browned. Serve warm.

**Phyllo dries out quickly and becomes brittle and hard to work with if not covered.*

TUSCAN WHITE BEAN CROSTINI

MAKES 18 CROSTINI

- **⅓ cup red wine vinegar**
- **3 tablespoons chopped fresh parsley**
- **1 tablespoon extra virgin olive oil**
- **2 cloves garlic, minced**
- **½ teaspoon dried oregano**
- **¼ teaspoon salt**
- **¼ teaspoon black pepper**
- **2 cans (about 15 ounces each) cannellini or Great Northern beans, rinsed and drained**
- **½ large red bell pepper, finely chopped *or* ⅓ cup finely chopped roasted red pepper**
- **⅓ cup finely chopped onion**
- **18 slices French bread, about ¼ inch thick**

1 Whisk vinegar, parsley, oil, garlic, oregano, salt and black pepper in large bowl until well blended. Add beans, bell pepper and onion; toss to coat. Cover and refrigerate 2 hours or overnight.

2 Preheat broiler. Arrange bread slices in single layer on large baking sheet or broiler pan. Broil 6 to 8 inches from heat 30 to 45 seconds or until lightly toasted. Cool completely.

3 Serve bean mixture on toast.

RISOTTO CROQUETTES

MAKES 4 TO 6 SERVINGS

- 3 tablespoons butter, divided
- 2 tablespoons all-purpose flour
- ¾ teaspoon salt, divided
- ½ cup milk
- 2 tablespoons grated Romano cheese
- Dash ground nutmeg
- 1 tablespoon extra virgin olive oil
- 1 onion, chopped
- 1 cup uncooked arborio rice
- 1 clove garlic, minced
- 3 tablespoons dry white wine
- 2¼ cups vegetable broth
- 3 tablespoons pine nuts, toasted*
- 2 tablespoons golden raisins
- 2 tablespoons chopped fresh basil
- ¼ teaspoon black pepper
- 3 cups Italian-seasoned bread crumbs
- 3 eggs
- 2 tablespoons cold water
- ½ cup vegetable oil

**To toast pine nuts, cook in medium skillet over medium heat 3 to 4 minutes or until lightly browned and fragrant, stirring frequently.*

1. For sauce, melt 2 tablespoons butter in small saucepan over medium heat. Whisk in flour and ¼ teaspoon salt until blended. Gradually whisk in milk; bring to a boil over high heat, stirring constantly. Reduce heat to low; simmer 2 to 3 minutes until slightly thickened. Remove from heat. Stir in cheese and nutmeg; set aside.
2. Meanwhile, heat remaining 1 tablespoon butter and olive oil in medium saucepan over medium heat until butter melts. Add onion; cook and stir about 3 minutes or until tender. Add rice and garlic; cook and stir until rice is coated. Add wine; cook and stir until liquid is absorbed.
3. Stir in broth and remaining ½ teaspoon salt. Bring to a boil over medium-high heat. Reduce heat to low; cover and simmer 20 minutes or until rice is tender and liquid is absorbed. Remove from heat. Cover; let stand 5 minutes.
4. Transfer mixture to large bowl. Stir in sauce, pine nuts, raisins, basil and pepper. Shape rice mixture by ¼-cupfuls into balls; flatten slightly. Place on waxed paper-lined baking sheet. Cover; refrigerate 1 hour.
5. Place bread crumbs in shallow bowl. Whisk eggs and water in another shallow bowl. Roll each croquette in bread crumbs, then in egg mixture, then in bread crumbs again. Return to waxed paper lined-baking sheet. Cover and refrigerate until ready to cook.
6. Heat vegetable oil in large deep skillet. Working in batches, carefully place six croquettes into oil. Cook about 45 seconds per side or until golden brown. Drain on paper towel-lined plate. Serve warm.

MEDITERRANEAN BAKED FETA

MAKES 4 TO 6 SERVINGS

- 1 block (8 ounces) feta cheese, cut crosswise into 4 slices
- ½ cup grape tomatoes, halved
- ¼ cup sliced roasted red peppers
- ¼ cup pitted Kalamata olives
- ⅛ teaspoon dried oregano
- Black pepper
- 2 tablespoons extra virgin olive oil
- 1 tablespoon shredded fresh basil
- Pita chips or pita bread wedges

1 Preheat oven to 400°F.

2 Place cheese in small baking dish; top with tomatoes, roasted peppers and olives. Sprinkle with oregano and season with black pepper; drizzle with oil.

3 Bake 12 minutes or until cheese is soft. Sprinkle with basil. Serve immediately with pita chips.

TIROKAFTERI (SPICY GREEK FETA SPREAD) ▸

MAKES 2 CUPS

- 2 small hot red peppers
- ½ small clove garlic
- 1 block (8 ounces) feta cheese
- ¾ cup plain Greek yogurt
- 1 tablespoon fresh lemon juice
- ½ teaspoon salt
- Crostini (page 5) and/or cut-up fresh vegetables

1 Preheat oven to 400°F. Place peppers on small piece of foil on baking sheet. Bake 15 minutes or until peppers are soft and charred. Cool completely. Scrape off skin with paring knife; cut off tops and remove seeds. Place peppers and garlic in food processor; pulse until finely chopped.

2 Add feta, yogurt, lemon juice and salt; pulse until well blended but still chunky. Serve with crostini and vegetables. Store in airtight container in refrigerator up to 2 weeks.

CAPRESE BRUSCHETTA

MAKES 12 SERVINGS

- ½ cup balsamic vinegar
- 6 plum tomatoes, seeded and diced
- 12 fresh basil leaves, chopped
- ¼ cup extra virgin olive oil
- 1 teaspoon salt
- Black pepper
- ¼ cup (½ stick) butter, softened
- 1 loaf French or Italian bread, cut into 24 slices
- Garlic powder
- 24 pearl-size balls (perlini) or cubes fresh mozzarella cheese

1 Bring vinegar to a simmer in small saucepan over medium heat. Reduce heat to low; cook 10 to 15 minutes or until mixture is reduced to a syrup, swirling pan frequently. Pour into small bowl.

2 Combine tomatoes, basil, oil and salt in medium bowl. Season to taste with pepper.

3 Preheat broiler. Spread butter over both sides of bread slices; sprinkle with garlic powder. Place on baking sheet. Broil about 1 minute per side or until crisp. Top bread slices with tomato mixture and cheese. Drizzle with balsamic syrup.

ROASTED PEPPER HUMMUS AND OLIVE TOASTS

MAKES 24 TOASTS

- **2 cloves garlic, peeled**
- **1 can (about 15 ounces) chickpeas, rinsed and drained**
- **1 cup chopped drained roasted red peppers**
- **¼ cup olive oil**
- **Salt and black pepper**
- **½ cup drained pitted black olives**
- **½ cup drained pimiento-stuffed green olives**
- **24 (½-inch) toasted French bread slices or Crostini (page 5)**

1 With motor running, drop garlic through feed tube of food processor; process until finely chopped. Add chickpeas and roasted peppers; process until paste forms. Add oil; process until smooth. Transfer to medium bowl; season with salt and black pepper. Cover and let stand 30 minutes to allow flavors to blend.

2 Place black and green olives in clean food processor; pulse until coarsely chopped.

3 Spread 2 tablespoons chickpea mixture on each bread slice. Spoon 1 tablespoon olive mixture in center of chickpea mixture. Serve at room temperature.

TIP

The hummus and olive mixtures can both be prepared up to 2 days in advance. Store separately in airtight containers in the refrigerator.

SALADS & VEGETABLES

MEDITERRANEAN SALAD

MAKES 4 SERVINGS

- 2 cups chopped iceberg lettuce
- 2 cups baby spinach
- 2 cups diced cucumbers
- 1 cup diced cooked chicken
- 1 cup chopped roasted red peppers
- 1 cup grape tomatoes, halved
- 1 cup quartered artichoke hearts
- ¾ cup crumbled feta cheese
- ½ cup chopped red onion
- 1 cup hummus
- ½ teaspoon Italian seasoning

1 Divide lettuce and spinach among four salad bowls or plates; top with cucumbers, chicken, roasted peppers, tomatoes, artichokes, cheese and onion.

2 Top salad with hummus; sprinkle with Italian seasoning.

MEDITERRANEAN-STYLE ROASTED VEGETABLES

MAKES 6 SERVINGS

- 1½ pounds red potatoes, cut into ½-inch chunks
- 2 tablespoons extra virgin olive oil, divided
- 1 red bell pepper, cut into ½-inch pieces
- 1 yellow or orange bell pepper, cut into ½-inch pieces
- 1 small red onion, cut into ½-inch wedges
- 2 cloves garlic, minced
- ½ teaspoon salt
- ¼ teaspoon black pepper
- 1 tablespoon balsamic vinegar
- ¼ cup chopped fresh basil

1. Preheat oven to 425°F. Spray large baking sheet with nonstick cooking spray.
2. Place potatoes on prepared baking sheet. Drizzle with 1 tablespoon oil; toss to coat evenly. Roast 10 minutes.
3. Add bell peppers and onion to baking sheet. Drizzle with remaining 1 tablespoon oil. Sprinkle with garlic, salt and black pepper; toss to coat evenly.
4. Roast 18 to 20 minutes or until vegetables are browned and tender, stirring once.
5. Transfer vegetables to large serving dish. Drizzle with vinegar; toss to coat evenly. Top with basil. Serve warm.

GREEK SALAD

MAKES 6 SERVINGS

SALAD

- 3 medium tomatoes, cut into 8 wedges each
- 1 green bell pepper, cut into 1-inch pieces
- ½ English cucumber (8 to 10 inches), quartered lengthwise and cut crosswise into ½-inch slices
- ½ red onion, thinly sliced
- ½ cup pitted Kalamata olives
- 1 block (8 ounces) feta cheese, cut into ½-inch cubes

DRESSING

- 6 tablespoons extra virgin olive oil
- 3 tablespoons red wine vinegar
- 1 to 2 cloves garlic, minced
- ¾ teaspoon dried oregano
- ¾ teaspoon salt
- ¼ teaspoon black pepper

1. For salad, combine tomatoes, bell pepper, cucumber, onion and olives in large bowl. Top with feta.

2. For dressing, whisk oil, vinegar, garlic, oregano, salt and black pepper in small bowl until well blended. Pour over salad; stir gently to coat.

GREEK LEMON POTATOES ▸

MAKES 4 SERVINGS

- 2½ pounds Yukon gold or yellow potatoes, peeled and cut into 1-inch pieces
- 3 tablespoons fresh lemon juice, divided
- 2 tablespoons extra virgin olive oil
- 2 teaspoons Greek seasoning
- Chopped fresh parsley (optional)

1 Preheat oven to 450°F. Spray baking sheet with nonstick cooking spray.

2 Combine potatoes, 2 tablespoons lemon juice, oil and Greek seasoning in large bowl; toss to coat. Spread potatoes in single layer on prepared baking sheet.

3 Roast about 25 minutes or until golden brown on bottom. Turn and bake 10 minutes or until tender and golden brown. Drizzle potatoes with remaining 1 tablespoon lemon juice; sprinkle with parsley, if desired.

MEDITERRANEAN VEGETABLE TIAN

MAKES 4 SERVINGS

- 2 tomatoes, sliced
- 1 small red onion, sliced
- 1 medium zucchini, sliced
- 1 small eggplant, sliced
- 1 small yellow squash, sliced
- 1 large portobello mushroom, sliced
- 3 tablespoons extra virgin olive oil
- 2 cloves garlic, minced
- 2 teaspoons chopped fresh rosemary leaves
- ⅔ cup dry white wine
- Salt and black pepper

1 Preheat oven to 350°F. Grease oval casserole dish or 13×9-inch baking dish.

2 Arrange slices of vegetables in rows, alternating different types and overlapping slices in baking dish to make attractive arrangement. Whisk oil, garlic and rosemary in small bowl; drizzle over vegetables. Pour wine over vegetables; season with salt and pepper. Cover loosely with foil.

3 Bake 20 minutes. Uncover; bake 10 to 15 minutes or until vegetables are tender.

RATATOUILLE

MAKES 6 TO 8 SERVINGS

- 2 tablespoons extra virgin olive oil
- 1 medium onion, chopped
- 2 red bell peppers, cut into 1-inch pieces
- 3 cloves garlic, minced
- 1 teaspoon Italian seasoning
- Pinch red pepper flakes
- 1 can (28 ounces) whole tomatoes, undrained, coarsely chopped or crushed with hands
- 1 medium eggplant (about 1 pound), cut into ½-inch pieces
- 3 small zucchini (about 12 ounces), cut in half lengthwise then cut crosswise into ¾-inch slices
- 1 fresh basil sprig
- 1 fresh rosemary sprig
- 1 tablespoon tomato paste
- 1½ teaspoons salt
- ¼ teaspoon black pepper
- 1 tablespoon balsamic or red wine vinegar
- ¼ cup chopped fresh basil

1 Heat oil in large saucepan or Dutch oven over medium-high heat. Add onion; cook and stir 2 minutes. Add bell peppers; cook and stir 3 minutes. Add garlic, Italian seasoning and red pepper flakes; cook and stir 30 seconds.

2 Stir in tomatoes with liquid, eggplant, zucchini, basil sprig, rosemary sprig, tomato paste, salt and black pepper; bring to a simmer. Reduce heat to medium-low; cover and simmer 30 minutes or until vegetables are tender.

3 Remove and discard herb sprigs. Stir in vinegar and chopped basil. Serve warm or at room temperature.

HOUSE SALAD

MAKES 4 SERVINGS

DRESSING

- ½ cup mayonnaise
- ½ cup white wine vinegar
- ¼ cup grated Parmesan cheese
- 1 tablespoon extra virgin olive oil
- 1 tablespoon fresh lemon juice
- 1 tablespoon honey
- 1 clove garlic, minced
- ¾ teaspoon Italian seasoning
- ½ teaspoon salt
- ½ teaspoon black pepper

SALAD

- 1 package (10 ounces) Italian salad blend
- 2 plum tomatoes, thinly sliced
- 1 cup croutons (purchased or homemade, recipe follows)
- ½ cup thinly sliced red or green bell pepper
- ½ cup thinly sliced red onion
- ¼ cup sliced black olives
- Pepperoncini peppers (optional)

1. For dressing, whisk mayonnaise, vinegar, cheese, oil, lemon juice, honey, garlic, Italian seasoning, salt and black pepper in medium bowl until well blended.

2. For salad, place salad blend in large bowl; top with tomatoes, croutons, bell pepper, onion, olives and pepperoncini, if desired. Add dressing; toss to coat.

HOMEMADE CROUTONS

Preheat oven to 350°F. Cut any kind of hearty bread into cubes (whole wheat, Tuscan or sourdough). Spread the bread on large baking sheet and drizzle with olive oil; toss to coat. If desired, season with salt and pepper and dried herbs like oregano, thyme or rosemary. Bake 10 to 15 minutes or until golden brown, stirring once or twice. Cool completely on baking sheet.

ITALIAN BREAD SALAD

MAKES 4 SERVINGS

- 3 slices (½-inch-thick) day-old whole wheat bread
- ½ cup buttermilk
- 1 clove garlic, minced
- 1 tablespoon minced fresh dill *or* 1 teaspoon dried dill weed
- 1½ teaspoons onion powder
- ¼ teaspoon black pepper
- 2 large tomatoes, cored and cut into 1-inch cubes
- 1 small cucumber, peeled, cut lengthwise into halves, seeded and thinly sliced
- 1 small stalk celery, thinly sliced
- 2 tablespoons minced fresh parsley
- ½ teaspoon salt

1. Preheat oven to 400°F. Cut bread into 1-inch pieces; place on baking sheet. Bake 5 to 7 minutes or until dry and lightly toasted, stirring occasionally. Cool completely on baking sheet.

2. For dressing, whisk buttermilk, garlic, dill, onion powder and pepper in small bowl until well blended. Let stand 15 minutes to allow flavors to blend.

3. Combine tomatoes, cucumber, celery and parsley in large bowl. Sprinkle with salt; toss well. Just before serving, stir in toasted bread. Whisk dressing; pour over salad and toss to coat. Serve immediately.

BROCCOLI ITALIAN STYLE ▸

MAKES 4 SERVINGS

- 1¼ pounds fresh broccoli
- 2 tablespoons fresh lemon juice
- 1 tablespoon extra virgin olive oil
- 1 tablespoon chopped fresh parsley
- 1 clove garlic, minced
- ½ teaspoon salt
- ¼ teaspoon black pepper

1. Trim broccoli, discarding tough stems. Cut broccoli into florets with 2-inch stems. Peel remaining stems; cut into ½-inch slices.
2. Bring large saucepan of salted water to a boil. Add broccoli; cook 3 to 5 minutes or until crisp-tender. Drain; transfer to serving dish.
3. Whisk lemon juice, oil, parsley, garlic, salt and pepper in small bowl. Pour over broccoli; toss to coat. Cover and let stand 1 hour before serving to allow flavors to blend. Serve at room temperature.

FETA-STUFFED TOMATOES

MAKES 4 SERVINGS

- 2 plum tomatoes, cut lengthwise into halves
- ⅓ cup chopped seeded cucumber
- 1 tablespoon crumbled feta cheese
- 1 tablespoon chopped fresh mint
- 1 tablespoon Greek yogurt
- ½ teaspoon grated lemon peel
- Salt and black pepper

1. Scoop out and discard pulp from tomatoes, leaving ¼-inch-thick shells. Place tomato shells cut sides down on paper towels to drain.
2. Combine cucumber, cheese, mint, yogurt and lemon peel; season with salt and pepper. Spoon mixture into tomato shells; serve immediately.

CREAMY LAYERED VEGETABLE BAKE

MAKES 8 SERVINGS

- 2 large eggplants
- 4 teaspoons salt, divided
- 5 tablespoons extra virgin olive oil, divided
- ½ teaspoon black pepper
- ½ cup chopped onion
- 2 medium zucchini, thinly sliced
- 1 package (8 ounces) sliced mushrooms
- 1 tablespoon Italian seasoning
- 2 teaspoons minced garlic, divided
- 1 container (15 ounces) ricotta cheese
- 1 cup shredded Parmesan cheese, divided
- 1 egg
- 12 ounces fresh mozzarella cheese, thinly sliced
- ¼ cup (½ stick) butter
- 3 tablespoons all-purpose flour
- 1¾ cups milk

1. Peel eggplants; cut off and discard ends. Cut each eggplant vertically into six equal slices. Place slices in large colander set over bowl; sprinkle with 2 teaspoons salt. Let stand 30 minutes. Rinse eggplant under cold water. Pat dry with paper towels.

2. Preheat oven to 400°F. Arrange eggplant slices in single layer on baking sheets. Brush both sides of slices evenly with 4 tablespoons oil; sprinkle with 1 teaspoon salt and pepper. Bake 20 minutes or until golden brown and tender, turning slices halfway through. *Reduce oven temperature to 350°F.*

3. Meanwhile, heat remaining 1 tablespoon oil in large skillet over medium heat. Add onion; cook and stir 3 minutes. Add zucchini, mushrooms, Italian seasoning, 1 teaspoon garlic and ½ teaspoon salt; cook and stir 5 to 7 minutes or until vegetables are tender.

4. Combine ricotta cheese, ½ cup Parmesan cheese and egg in medium bowl; mix well.

5. Spray 13×9-inch baking dish with nonstick cooking spray. Arrange eggplant slices in single layer in prepared dish. Layer with half of mozzarella cheese, half of zucchini mixture and half of ricotta mixture. Repeat layers.

6. Melt butter in medium saucepan over medium heat. Add remaining 1 teaspoon garlic; cook and stir 1 minute. Whisk in flour; cook 1 minute. Gradually whisk in milk; whisk 2 to 3 minutes or until sauce is thickened. Season with remaining ½ teaspoon salt. Pour sauce evenly over vegetables and cheese. Top with remaining ½ cup Parmesan cheese.

7 Bake 30 minutes or until heated through and cheese is melted. Let stand 10 to 15 minutes before serving.

MARINATED ANTIPASTO

MAKES ABOUT 4 SERVINGS

- ¼ cup extra virgin olive oil
- 2 tablespoons balsamic vinegar
- 1 clove garlic, minced
- ½ teaspoon sugar
- ½ teaspoon salt
- ¼ teaspoon black pepper
- 1 pint (2 cups) cherry tomatoes
- 1 can (about 14 ounces) quartered artichoke hearts, drained
- 8 ounces pearl-size balls (perlini) or cubes fresh mozzarella cheese
- 1 cup drained pitted Kalamata olives
- ¼ cup sliced fresh basil
- Bibb lettuce leaves

1. Whisk oil, vinegar, garlic, sugar, salt and pepper in large bowl until well blended. Add tomatoes, artichokes, cheese, olives and basil; toss to coat. Let stand at room temperature 30 minutes.

2. Line platter or serving plates with lettuce. Arrange antipasto over lettuce; serve at room temperature.

SERVING SUGGESTION

Serve antipasto with toothpicks as an appetizer or spoon over lettuce leaves for a first-course salad.

MEDITERRANEAN PASTA SALAD

MAKES 6 SERVINGS

- 6 ounces uncooked farfalle (bowtie) pasta
- 1 can (about 15 ounces) chickpeas, rinsed and drained
- 1 can (about 14 ounces) artichoke hearts, rinsed, drained and quartered
- 1 cup sliced zucchini, halved
- ¼ cup chopped red onion
- ¼ cup fresh lemon juice
- ¼ cup extra virgin olive oil
- 1 clove garlic, minced
- ½ teaspoon salt
- ½ teaspoon Italian seasoning
- ¼ teaspoon black pepper
- ¼ cup crumbled feta cheese

1. Cook pasta in large saucepan of boiling salted water according to package directions for al dente. Drain; cool completely.

2. Combine pasta, chickpeas, artichokes, zucchini and onion in large bowl.

3. Whisk lemon juice, oil, garlic, salt, Italian seasoning and pepper in small bowl until well blended. Drizzle over pasta mixture; toss to coat. Top with cheese before serving.

GREEK LEMON AND RICE SOUP

MAKES 4 SERVINGS

- 4 cups chicken broth
- ½ cup uncooked long-grain rice
- 3 egg yolks
- ¼ cup fresh lemon juice
- Salt and black pepper
- Finely chopped fresh parsley (optional)

SLOW COOKER DIRECTIONS

1 Combine broth and rice in slow cooker. Cover and cook on HIGH 2 to 3 hours or until rice is tender and fully cooked.

2 *Turn slow cooker to LOW.* Whisk egg yolks and lemon juice in medium bowl. Stir large spoonful of hot rice mixture into egg yolk mixture; stir mixture back into rice mixture in slow cooker. Cover; cook on LOW 10 minutes.

3 Season with salt and pepper. Garnish with parsley.

MEDITERRANEAN LAMB STEW

MAKES 4 SERVINGS

- 1 pound lamb shoulder or stew meat, cut into 1-inch pieces
- Salt and black pepper
- 3 tablespoons extra virgin olive oil
- 1 medium red onion, chopped
- 2 cloves garlic, minced
- 1 teaspoon dried rosemary
- ½ teaspoon dried oregano
- 1 can (about 14 ounces) diced tomatoes with green chiles
- 1 can (about 15 ounces) cannellini beans, rinsed and drained
- Tzatziki Sauce (recipe follows; optional)

1 Season lamb all over with salt and pepper. Heat oil in large saucepan over medium heat. Add lamb; cook until browned on all sides. Transfer lamb to bowl. Add onion to drippings in skillet; cook and stir 5 minutes or until softened. Add garlic, rosemary and oregano; cook and stir 1 minute.

2 Return lamb and any accumulated juices to saucepan; stir in tomatoes and beans. Bring to a simmer. Reduce heat to medium-low; partially cover and simmer about 1 hour or until lamb is tender. Season with additional salt and pepper. Serve with Tzatziki Sauce, if desired.

TZATZIKI SAUCE

Stir 1 cup Greek yogurt, ½ cup diced or shredded cucumber, 1 tablespoon lemon juice, ½ teaspoon lemon peel, ½ teaspoon garlic and ¼ teaspoon salt in small bowl until combined. Cover and refrigerate until ready to use.

LENTIL SOUP

MAKES 6 TO 8 SERVINGS

- **2 tablespoons extra virgin olive oil, divided**
- **2 medium onions, chopped**
- **1½ teaspoons salt**
- **4 cloves garlic, minced**
- **¼ cup tomato paste**
- **1 teaspoon dried oregano**
- **½ teaspoon dried basil**
- **¼ teaspoon dried thyme**
- **¼ teaspoon black pepper**
- **½ cup dry sherry or white wine**
- **8 cups vegetable broth**
- **2 cups water**
- **3 carrots, cut into ½-inch pieces**
- **2 cups dried lentils, rinsed and sorted**
- **1 cup chopped fresh parsley**
- **1 tablespoon balsamic vinegar**

1. Heat 1 tablespoon oil in large saucepan or Dutch oven over medium heat. Add onions; cook 10 minutes, stirring occasionally. Add remaining 1 tablespoon oil and salt; cook 10 minutes or until onions are golden brown, stirring frequently.
2. Add garlic; cook and stir 1 minute. Add tomato paste, oregano, basil, thyme and pepper; cook and stir 1 minute. Stir in sherry; cook 30 seconds, stirring to scrape up browned bits.
3. Stir in broth, water, carrots and lentils; cover and bring to a boil over high heat. Reduce heat to medium-low; partially cover and cook 30 minutes or until lentils are tender.
4. Remove from heat; stir in parsley and vinegar.

BEAN SOUP PROVENÇALE

MAKES 8 TO 10 SERVINGS

- Pesto Sauce (recipe follows)
- ¼ cup extra virgin olive oil
- 1½ cups chopped onion
- 1½ cups chopped celery
- 1 cup sliced leeks
- 8 cups water
- 1 cup sliced carrots
- 1 turnip, peeled and diced
- 1 teaspoon salt
- ¼ teaspoon black pepper
- 2 cans (about 15 ounces each) Great Northern beans, rinsed and drained
- 1 small zucchini, sliced
- 1 cup sliced fresh or chopped spinach

1 Prepare Pesto Sauce; set aside.

2 Heat oil in large saucepan over medium heat. Add onion, celery and leeks; cook and stir 10 minutes or until onion is soft.

3 Add water, carrots, turnip, salt and pepper; bring to a boil over high heat. Reduce heat to low; cover and simmer 30 minutes or until vegetables are tender.

4 Add beans, zucchini and spinach; cook until heated through. Top with Pesto Sauce.

PESTO SAUCE

Combine ½ cup fresh parsley leaves, ½ cup fresh basil leaves, ¼ cup grated Parmesan cheese, ¼ cup extra virgin olive oil, 2 cloves garlic and ½ teaspoon salt in food processor or blender; process until smooth. Makes about ⅓ cup.

FRENCH PEASANT SOUP

MAKES 4 SERVINGS

- 2 tablespoons extra virgin olive oil
- 1 cup diced carrot
- 1 cup diced celery
- 1 onion, chopped
- 2 cloves garlic, minced
- ¼ cup dry white wine or water
- 4 cups vegetable broth
- 1 bay leaf
- 1 fresh thyme sprig *or* 1 teaspoon dried thyme
- 1 fresh parsley sprig *or* 1 teaspoon dried parsley flakes
- 1 cup chopped green beans (½-inch pieces)
- ½ cup uncooked small pasta or elbow macaroni
- 1 can (about 15 ounces) cannellini beans, rinsed and drained
- 1 cup diced zucchini
- 1 leek, chopped
- 4 teaspoons prepared pesto (jarred or homemade, page 54)
- Shredded Parmesan cheese

1 Heat oil in large saucepan over medium heat. Add carrot, celery, onion and garlic; cook 5 minutes or until carrots are crisp-tender. Stir in wine; cook until most of wine has evaporated. Add broth, bay leaf, thyme and parsley; cook 10 minutes.

2 Add green beans to saucepan; cook 5 minutes. Add pasta; cook 5 to 7 minutes or until almost tender. Add cannellini beans, zucchini and leek; cook 3 to 5 minutes or until vegetables are tender.

3 Remove and discard bay leaf and herb sprigs. Ladle soup into bowls. Stir 1 teaspoon pesto into each bowl; sprinkle with cheese.

TUSCAN WHITE BEAN SOUP

MAKES 8 TO 10 SERVINGS

- 10 cups chicken broth
- 1 package (16 ounces) dried Great Northern beans, rinsed and sorted
- 1 can (about 14 ounces) diced tomatoes
- 1 large onion, chopped
- 3 carrots, chopped
- 6 ounces bacon, crisp-cooked and chopped
- 4 cloves garlic, minced
- 1 sprig fresh rosemary *or* 1 teaspoon dried rosemary
- 1 teaspoon salt
- 1 teaspoon black pepper

SLOW COOKER DIRECTIONS

1. Combine broth, beans, tomatoes, onion, carrots, bacon, garlic, rosemary, salt and pepper in slow cooker.
2. Cover; cook on LOW 8 hours. Remove and discard rosemary before serving.

SERVING SUGGESTION

Place slices of toasted Italian bread in soup bowls; drizzle with olive oil. Ladle soup over bread.

GRAINS & BEANS

CHICKPEA AND SPINACH BOWLS

MAKES 4 SERVINGS

- 4 cups packed baby spinach
- 1 can (about 15 ounces) chickpeas, rinsed and drained
- 1 large shallot, thinly sliced
- 4 pitted Kalamata olives, sliced
- 2 tablespoons crumbled feta cheese
- ¼ cup plain Greek yogurt
- 2 teaspoons white wine vinegar
- 1 clove garlic, minced
- 1 tablespoon extra virgin olive oil
- ½ teaspoon salt
- ¼ teaspoon black pepper

1. Combine spinach, chickpeas, shallot, olives and cheese in large bowl; toss gently.
2. Whisk yogurt, vinegar, garlic, oil, salt and pepper in small bowl until well blended. Add to salad just before serving; toss gently.

GREEK GIANT BEANS IN TOMATO SAUCE

MAKES ABOUT 8 SERVINGS

- 1 pound dried gigante beans* (about 2¼ cups), soaked 8 hours or overnight
- 1½ tablespoons salt, divided
- 2 bay leaves
- ¼ cup extra virgin olive oil
- 2 small onions, chopped
- 1 stalk celery, finely chopped
- 1 medium carrot, finely chopped
- 3 cloves garlic, minced
- 2 tablespoons tomato paste
- 1 teaspoon dried oregano, plus additional for serving
- ½ teaspoon black pepper
- ⅛ teaspoon red pepper flakes
- 1 can (28 ounces) whole tomatoes, undrained, coarsely chopped or crushed with hands**
- Chopped fresh parsley
- Crumbled feta cheese

**If gigante beans are not available, use another variety of large white beans such as lima, butter or corona beans.*

***Or substitute 1 can (28 ounces) diced tomatoes.*

1. Combine beans, 6 cups water, 1 tablespoon salt and bay leaves in large saucepan. Bring to a boil over high heat. Reduce heat to medium-low; simmer 1 hour or until beans are tender enough to bite but not completely cooked.

2. Meanwhile, heat oil in medium saucepan over medium-high heat. Add onion, celery, carrot and garlic; cook and stir 8 minutes or until vegetables are tender. Add tomato paste, remaining 1½ teaspoons salt, oregano, black pepper and red pepper flakes; cook and stir 1 minute. Stir in tomatoes; remove from heat.

3. Preheat oven to 350°F. Drain beans, discarding bay leaves and any loose bean skins, reserving 2 cups cooking water. Combine beans, reserved water and tomato sauce in large bowl. Spread in 13×9-inch baking dish. Bake about 2 hours or until beans are tender and creamy, stirring every 30 minutes.

4. Top with parsley, cheese and additional oregano.

MUJADARA

MAKES 6 SERVINGS

- **1 cup dried lentils, rinsed and sorted**
- **¼ cup plus 1 tablespoon extra virgin olive oil, divided**
- **3 sweet onions, thinly sliced**
- **2½ teaspoons salt, divided**
- **1½ teaspoons ground cumin**
- **1 teaspoon ground allspice**
- **1 cinnamon stick**
- **1 bay leaf**
- **⅛ to ¼ teaspoon ground red pepper**
- **¾ cup uncooked long grain rice, rinsed and drained**
- **3 cups vegetable broth or water**
- **1 cucumber**
- **1 cup plain Greek yogurt or sour cream**

1. Place lentils in medium saucepan; cover with water by 1 inch. Bring to a boil over medium-high heat. Reduce heat to medium-low; simmer 10 minutes. Drain and rinse under cold water.

2. Meanwhile, heat ¼ cup oil in large saucepan or Dutch oven over medium heat. Add onions and 1 teaspoon salt; cook and stir 15 minutes or until golden brown and parts are crispy. Remove most of onions to small bowl, leaving about ½ cup in saucepan.*

3. Add remaining 1 tablespoon oil to saucepan with onions; heat over medium-high heat. Add cumin, allspice, cinnamon stick, bay leaf and red pepper; cook and stir 30 seconds. Add rice; cook and stir 2 to 3 minutes or until rice is lightly toasted. Stir in broth, lentils and 1 teaspoon salt; bring to a boil. Reduce heat to low; cover and cook about 15 minutes or until broth is absorbed and rice and lentils are tender. Remove saucepan from heat. Place clean kitchen towel over top of saucepan; replace lid and let stand 5 to 10 minutes.

4. Meanwhile, peel cucumber and trim ends. Grate cucumber on large holes of box grater; squeeze out excess liquid. Place in medium bowl; stir in yogurt and remaining ½ teaspoon salt. Serve lentils and rice with reserved onions and cucumber sauce.

**If desired, continue to cook reserved onions in medium skillet over medium heat until dark golden brown.*

RISOTTO ALLA MILANESE

MAKES 6 TO 8 SERVINGS

- ¼ teaspoon saffron threads
- 5 cups vegetable or chicken broth
- 4 tablespoons butter, divided
- 1 large onion, chopped
- 1½ cups uncooked arborio rice
- ½ cup dry white wine
- ½ teaspoon salt
- Dash black pepper
- ¼ cup grated Parmesan cheese
- Chopped fresh parsley (optional)

1. Crush saffron to a powder; place in glass measuring cup.

2. Bring broth to a boil in medium saucepan over medium heat; reduce heat to low. Stir ½ cup broth into saffron to dissolve; set aside. Keep remaining broth hot.

3. Heat 3 tablespoons butter in large saucepan over medium heat until melted and bubbly. Add onion; cook and stir 5 minutes or until onion is softened. Add rice; cook and stir 2 minutes. Stir in wine, salt and pepper; cook over medium-high heat 3 to 5 minutes until wine is absorbed, stirring occasionally.

4. Reduce heat to medium-low. Stir ½ cup hot broth into rice mixture; cook and stir until broth is absorbed. Repeat, adding ½ cup broth three more times, cooking and stirring until broth is absorbed.

5. Add saffron-flavored broth to rice; cook until absorbed. Continue to add remaining broth, ½ cup at a time, cooking and stirring until rice is tender but firm and mixture has slight creamy consistency. (Not all broth may be necessary. Total cooking time will be 20 to 25 minutes.)

6. Remove risotto from heat. Stir in remaining 1 tablespoon butter and cheese. Sprinkle with parsley, if desired. Serve immediately.

SPANISH RICE ▸

MAKES 6 TO 8 SERVINGS

- 1 tablespoon extra virgin olive oil
- 1 small onion, chopped
- 2 cloves garlic, minced
- 2 cups uncooked brown rice, rinsed well and drained
- 3½ cups water or chicken broth
- 1 can (about 14 ounces) diced tomatoes with green chiles
- 1½ teaspoons salt

1. Heat oil in medium saucepan over medium-high heat. Add onion and garlic; cook and stir 2 minutes. Add rice; cook and stir 2 minutes.
2. Stir in water, tomatoes and salt; bring to a boil. Reduce heat to low; cover and simmer 35 to 40 minutes or until rice is tender and water is absorbed. Fluff rice with fork.

PESTO RICE AND BEANS

MAKES 8 SERVINGS

- 1½ cups vegetable broth or water
- ¾ cup uncooked long grain white rice
- 1½ cups frozen cut green beans
- 1 can (about 15 ounces) Great Northern beans, rinsed and drained
- ½ cup pesto (jarred or homemade, page 54)
- ½ cup grated Parmesan cheese

1. Bring broth to a boil in medium saucepan. Add rice; reduce heat to low. Cover and cook 12 to 15 minutes or until rice is tender.
2. Meanwhile, cook green beans according to package directions.
3. Stir green beans and Great Northern beans into rice. Stir in pesto and cheese. Let stand, covered, 5 minutes or until cheese is melted. Serve immediately.

PARMESAN POLENTA

MAKES 6 SERVINGS

- **4 cups vegetable broth**
- **1 small onion, minced**
- **4 cloves garlic, minced**
- **1 tablespoon minced fresh rosemary *or* 1 teaspoon dried rosemary**
- **½ teaspoon salt**
- **1¼ cups yellow cornmeal**
- **6 tablespoons grated Parmesan cheese**
- **1 tablespoon extra virgin olive oil, divided**

1. Spray 11×7-inch baking pan with nonstick cooking spray. Spray one side of 7-inch-long sheet of waxed paper with cooking spray.

2. Combine broth, onion, garlic, rosemary and salt in medium saucepan; bring to a boil over high heat. Gradually add cornmeal, stirring constantly. Reduce heat to medium; simmer 30 minutes or until mixture has consistency of thick mashed potatoes, stirring frequently. Remove from heat; stir in cheese.

3. Spread polenta evenly in prepared pan. Place waxed paper, sprayed side down, on polenta; smooth surface. (If surface is bumpy, it is more likely to stick to grill.) Cool on wire rack 15 minutes or until firm. Remove waxed paper; cut into six squares.

4. Spray grid with cooking spray. Prepare grill for direct cooking. Brush tops of polenta squares with half of oil. Grill polenta, oil side down, covered, over medium-low heat 6 to 8 minutes or until golden brown. Brush with remaining oil; turn and grill 6 to 8 minutes or until golden brown. Serve warm.

BULGUR SALAD NIÇOISE

MAKES 4 SERVINGS

- 2 cups water
- ¼ teaspoon salt
- 1 cup uncooked bulgur wheat
- 1 cup halved cherry tomatoes
- 1 can (6 ounces) tuna packed in water, drained and flaked
- ½ cup pitted black niçoise olives*
- 3 tablespoons finely chopped green onion
- 1 tablespoon slivered fresh mint
- 2 tablespoons fresh lemon juice
- 1 tablespoon extra virgin olive oil
- ⅛ teaspoon black pepper

***If you use larger olives, slice or chop as desired.**

1 Bring water and salt to a boil in medium saucepan. Stir in bulgur. Remove from heat; cover and let stand 10 to 15 minutes or until water is absorbed and bulgur is tender. Fluff with fork; set aside to cool completely.

2 Combine bulgur, tomatoes, tuna, olives, green onions and chopped mint in large bowl. Whisk lemon juice, oil and pepper in small bowl until blended. Pour dressing over salad; toss gently to coat.

RICE PRIMAVERA

MAKES 6 SERVINGS

- 3 tablespoons extra virgin olive oil, divided
- 1 zucchini, thinly sliced
- 1 onion, halved and thinly sliced
- 1 red bell pepper, thinly sliced
- 1 package (8 ounces) cremini mushrooms, stemmed and thinly sliced
- 1 cup uncooked long grain rice
- ¼ cup dry white wine
- ½ teaspoon salt
- 3 cups vegetable broth or water
- ½ cup grated Parmesan cheese
- Black pepper

1 Heat 1 tablespoon oil in large saucepan over medium heat. Add zucchini; cook and stir 5 minutes or until crisp-tender. Transfer to medium bowl.

2 Heat remaining 2 tablespoons oil in same saucepan over medium heat. Add onion, bell pepper and mushrooms; cook and stir 5 minutes or until bell pepper is crisp-tender. Add rice; cook and stir 1 minute. Add wine and salt; cook and stir until wine is absorbed. Add broth; bring to a boil over high heat. Reduce heat to medium-low; cook about 20 minutes or until rice is tender, stirring frequently.

3 Stir in cheese until melted. Stir in zucchini. Season to taste with black pepper.

POLENTA WITH MUSHROOM SAUCE

MAKES 6 SERVINGS

POLENTA

- 5 cups water
- 1 tablespoon sugar
- 1 teaspoon salt
- 1 cup yellow cornmeal
- ½ cup grated Parmesan or Romano cheese

MUSHROOM SAUCE

- 2 tablespoons extra virgin olive oil
- 1 large red onion, diced
- 2 pounds white or cremini mushrooms (or a combination), cut into thick slices
- ½ teaspoon salt
- ½ teaspoon dried thyme
- ½ teaspoon dried sage
- ½ teaspoon black pepper
- 1 teaspoon minced garlic
- 1 tablespoon all-purpose flour
- 1 cup dry white wine or vegetable broth

1 Preheat oven to 350°F.

2 For polenta, combine water, sugar and 1 teaspoon salt in Dutch oven or large ovenproof saucepan; bring to a boil over medium-high heat. Gradually whisk in cornmeal. Reduce heat to low; cook 5 minutes or until thickened, stirring frequently. Cover tightly; bake 1 hour. Stir in cheese.

3 Meanwhile for mushroom sauce, heat oil in large skillet over medium-high heat. Add onion; cook and stir 5 minutes or until soft. Add mushrooms; cook and stir until browned. Stir in ½ teaspoon salt, thyme, sage and pepper; cook 1 minute. Add garlic; cook and stir 1 minute. Sprinkle with flour; cook 1 minute, stirring constantly. Add wine; cook and stir until sauce thickens. Reduce heat to low; cover and simmer 15 minutes, stirring occasionally.

4 Divide polenta among six bowls; top with mushroom sauce.

PASTA & COUSCOUS

PASTA ALL'ARRABBIATA

MAKES 4 SERVINGS

- 3 tablespoons extra virgin olive oil
- 2 cloves garlic, minced
- 1 teaspoon crushed red pepper flakes
- 1 can (28 ounces) whole tomatoes, chopped and juice reserved
- ½ teaspoon salt
- 12 ounces uncooked spaghetti
- Finely chopped fresh parsley and/or grated Parmesan cheese

1. Heat oil in large saucepan over medium-low heat. Add garlic and pepper flakes; cook and stir 1 minute or until fragrant but not browned. Stir in tomatoes with juice and salt; cook 20 minutes or until thickened and flavors have blended, stirring occasionally.

2. Cook pasta in large saucepan of salted boiling water according to package directions for al dente. Drain, reserving 1 cup pasta cooking water.

3. Add pasta to sauce; stir to coat, adding reserved pasta water if necessary to loosen sauce. Serve topped with parsley.

CAPELLINI PRIMAVERA

MAKES 6 SERVINGS

- ¼ cup (½ stick) butter
- 1 cup chopped onion
- 1 cup julienned or shredded carrots
- 4 cups (1-inch) broccoli florets (2 small heads)
- 1 package (8 ounces) sliced mushrooms
- 1 yellow squash, halved lengthwise and thinly sliced (about 2 cups)
- 2 teaspoons minced garlic
- 1 teaspoon salt
- 1 can (about 14 ounces) crushed tomatoes
- ½ cup drained oil-packed sun-dried tomatoes, finely chopped
- 1 tablespoon finely chopped fresh parsley
- ½ teaspoon dried oregano
- ½ teaspoon dried rosemary
- ⅛ teaspoon red pepper flakes
- 12 ounces uncooked angel hair pasta (capellini)
- 2 tablespoons extra virgin olive oil
- Black pepper
- Grated Parmesan cheese (optional)

1. Melt butter in large skillet over medium-high heat. Add onion and carrots; cook and stir 3 minutes or until onion is softened. Add broccoli, mushrooms, squash, garlic and 1 teaspoon salt; cook 10 minutes or until mushrooms are tender, stirring frequently.

2. Reduce heat to medium-low. Add crushed tomatoes, sun-dried tomatoes, parsley, oregano, rosemary and red pepper flakes; cook 10 minutes, stirring occasionally.

3. Meanwhile, cook pasta in large saucepan of salted boiling water according to package directions for al dente. Drain and place in large bowl, reserving ½ cup pasta cooking water.

4. Stir reserved pasta cooking water into sauce; add sauce to pasta and toss to coat. Drizzle with oil; stir gently to coat. Season with additional salt and black pepper; serve with cheese, if desired.

VEGETABLE COUSCOUS ▸

MAKES 4 SERVINGS

- 2 tablespoons butter
- 1 onion, chopped
- 2 stalks celery, chopped
- 1 carrot, chopped
- 3 cups vegetable broth or water
- 1 package (about 8 ounces) uncooked pearl couscous
- ½ teaspoon salt
- ½ cup pine nuts or slivered almonds, toasted*

**To toast pine nuts, cook in medium skillet over medium heat 3 to 4 minutes or until lightly browned and fragrant, stirring frequently.*

1 Melt butter in medium saucepan over medium heat. Add onion, celery and carrot; cook and stir 5 minutes or until onion is translucent. Stir in broth, couscous and salt; bring to a boil over medium-high heat. Reduce heat to medium; simmer 10 minutes or until couscous is tender.

2 Fluff couscous with fork. Stir in nuts.

PARMESAN VEGETABLE COUSCOUS

Stir in ½ cup grated Parmesan cheese with the nuts.

PASTA PEPERONATA

MAKES 4 TO 6 SERVINGS

- 2 tablespoons extra virgin olive oil
- 4 cups sliced green, red and yellow bell peppers (about 1 of each color)
- 4 cups sliced onions
- 3 cloves garlic, minced
- 1 teaspoon dried basil
- ½ teaspoon dried marjoram leaves
- 8 ounces uncooked spaghetti or linguine
- Grated Parmesan cheese

1 Heat oil in large skillet over medium heat. Add bell peppers, onions, garlic, basil and marjoram; cover and cook 8 to 10 minutes or until vegetables are very tender. Uncover; cook and stir 20 to 30 minutes or until onions are golden brown and mixture is creamy.

2 Meanwhile, cook pasta in large saucepan of salted boiling water according to package directions for al dente. Drain.

3 Spoon pasta onto plates; top evenly with peperonata and cheese.

SPAGHETTI ALLA CARBONARA

MAKES 4 SERVINGS

- **12 ounces uncooked spaghetti**
- **3 eggs**
- **1 cup (about 2 ounces) lightly packed shredded Parmesan cheese**
- **¼ teaspoon salt**
- **Black pepper**
- **2 tablespoons extra virgin olive oil**
- **6 ounces guanciale or bacon, cut into ½-inch pieces**
- **1 clove garlic, minced**
- **Finely chopped fresh parsley**

1 Cook pasta in large saucepan of salted boiling water according to package directions for al dente. Drain, reserving 1 cup pasta cooking water.

2 Meanwhile, whisk eggs in medium bowl. Stir in cheese and salt; season with pepper. Heat oil in large skillet over medium heat. Add guanciale; cook about 5 minutes or until well browned on all sides, turning occasionally. Add garlic; cook and stir 1 minute.

3 Reduce heat to low; add pasta to skillet with ½ cup pasta cooking water. Gradually add small amounts of cheese mixture, stirring vigorously with wooden spoon or tongs until sauce is glossy and coats pasta, adding additional pasta water if needed to make smooth, glossy sauce. Taste and season with additional salt and black pepper. Serve immediately topped with parsley.

ORECCHIETTE WITH SAUSAGE AND BROCCOLI RABE

MAKES 4 TO 6 SERVINGS

- **1 tablespoon extra virgin olive oil**
- **12 ounces bulk mild Italian sausage**
- **3 cloves garlic, minced**
- **¼ teaspoon red pepper flakes**
- **4 cups chicken broth, divided**
- **¾ teaspoon salt**
- **1 package (16 ounces) uncooked orecchiette pasta**
- **1 bunch broccoli rabe (about 1 pound), tough stems removed, cut into 2-inch-long pieces**
- **¾ cup grated Parmesan cheese, divided**
- **Juice of 1 lemon**

1. Heat oil in large saucepan or Dutch oven over medium-high heat. Add sausage; cook about 8 minutes or until browned, stirring to break up meat. Add garlic and red pepper flakes; cook and stir 1 minute. Add 2 tablespoons broth, cook 1 minute, stirring to scrape up browned bits.

2. Stir in remaining broth and salt; bring to a boil. Add pasta, stirring to separate pieces as much as possible. Reduce heat to medium; cover and cook 10 minutes, stirring occasionally to prevent pasta from sticking.

3. Add broccoli rabe; stir to wilt and blend with pasta. Cover and cook 4 minutes or until pasta is tender and liquid is absorbed, stirring occasionally.

4. Stir in ½ cup cheese and lemon juice; mix well. Serve immediately with remaining ¼ cup cheese.

BUCATINI ALL'AMATRICIANA ▸

MAKES 4 SERVINGS

- 6 ounces guanciale or bacon, cut into ½-inch pieces
- 1 to 3 tablespoons extra virgin olive oil (optional)
- 1 onion, chopped
- 1 can (28 ounces) whole tomatoes, chopped and juice reserved
- ¼ teaspoon salt
- 12 ounces uncooked bucatini or spaghetti
- Grated Parmesan cheese (optional)

1 Cook guanciale in large saucepan over medium heat until well browned, turning occasionally; add oil if needed to make at least 3 tablespoons fat in saucepan. Add onion; cook and stir 5 minutes or until onion is translucent. Add tomatoes with juice and salt. Reduce heat to medium-low; simmer 20 to 30 minutes or until reduced slightly and flavors have blended.

2 Meanwhile, cook pasta in large saucepan of salted boiling water according to package directions for al dente. Drain, reserving 1 cup pasta cooking water. Add pasta to sauce; add pasta water by tablespoonfuls to make glossy sauce that coats pasta. Serve immediately topped with cheese, if desired.

MEDITERRANEAN PESTO ORZO WITH ARTICHOKES

MAKES 6 TO 8 SERVINGS

- 1 package (16 ounces) uncooked orzo pasta
- 2 cups lightly packed fresh basil leaves
- ½ cup whole almonds
- 4 cloves garlic
- ¼ teaspoon salt
- ¾ cup extra virgin olive oil
- 1 cup shredded Parmesan cheese, divided
- 1 jar (about 6 ounces) marinated artichoke hearts, drained and cut in half
- ½ cup pitted Kalamata olives

1 Cook pasta in large saucepan of salted boiling water according to package directions for al dente. Drain and place in large bowl.

2 Meanwhile for pesto, combine basil, almonds, garlic and salt in food processor; pulse until coarsely chopped. With motor running, pour in oil in thin steady stream; process until well blended and nuts are finely chopped. Add ½ cup cheese; pulse just until blended. Pour sauce over orzo; mix well.

3 Add artichokes, olives and remaining ½ cup cheese; fold until mixed. Serve immediately or cover and refrigerate until ready to serve.

SPINACH GNOCCHI

MAKES 4 TO 6 SERVINGS (ABOUT 32 GNOCCHI)

- 2 packages (10 ounces each) frozen chopped spinach
- 1 cup ricotta cheese
- 2 eggs
- ⅓ cup grated Parmesan cheese
- 3 tablespoons all-purpose flour
- ½ teaspoon salt
- ⅛ teaspoon black pepper
- ⅛ teaspoon ground nutmeg
- Marinara sauce, heated
- Shaved Parmesan cheese

1 Cook spinach according to package directions. Drain well; let cool. Squeeze spinach dry; place in medium bowl. Stir in ricotta, eggs, grated Parmesan cheese, flour, salt, pepper and nutmeg; mix well. Cover and refrigerate 1 hour.

2 Line baking sheet with parchment paper. Press heaping tablespoonful of spinach mixture between spoon and your hand to form oval gnocchi; place on prepared baking sheet. Repeat with remaining spinach mixture. Freeze gnocchi 30 minutes.

3 Bring large saucepan of salted water to a boil. Drop 8 to 12 gnocchi into boiling water; cook about 2½ minutes or until gnocchi float to surface. Remove gnocchi with slotted spoon; drain on paper towels. Return water to a boil; repeat with remaining gnocchi.

4 Serve gnocchi with marinara sauce and shaved Parmesan cheese.

CACIO E PEPE

MAKES 4 SERVINGS

- **12 ounces uncooked bucatini or spaghetti**
- **2 tablespoons extra virgin olive oil**
- **1 tablespoon black pepper, divided**
- **1 cup (about 2 ounces) lightly packed shredded Parmesan cheese**
- **1 cup (about 2 ounces) lightly packed shredded Pecorino Romano cheese***

Or substitute with additional Parmesan cheese instead.

1 Cook pasta in large saucepan of salted boiling water according to package directions for al dente. Drain, reserving 2 cups pasta cooking water.

2 Heat oil in large saucepan over medium heat. Add 2 teaspoons pepper; cook and stir 1 minute. Add pasta and ½ cup cooking water. Remove from heat. Gradually sprinkle in cheese by small handfuls, stirring vigorously with wooden spoon or tongs to make smooth sauce. Stir in additional pasta water as needed until sauce is smooth and glossy. Sprinkle with remaining 1 teaspoon pepper; serve immediately.

SPICY TOMATO VODKA PENNE

MAKES 4 TO 6 SERVINGS

- 1 package (16 ounces) uncooked penne pasta
- 6 tablespoons extra virgin olive oil
- 1 shallot, minced
- 2 cloves garlic, minced
- 1 can (6 ounces) tomato paste
- 2 tablespoons vodka
- ½ cup whipping cream
- 1 teaspoon red pepper flakes
- ½ teaspoon salt
- ¼ teaspoon black pepper
- 2 tablespoons butter
- ½ cup grated Parmesan cheese, plus additional for serving
- Shredded fresh basil

1. Cook pasta in large saucepan of salted boiling water according to package directions for al dente. Drain, reserving ½ cup pasta cooking water; return pasta to saucepan.

2. Meanwhile, heat oil in large saucepan over medium heat. Add shallot and garlic; cook and stir 3 to 5 minutes or until soft. Add tomato paste; cook and stir 5 minutes. Add vodka; cook and stir until evaporated. Stir in cream, red pepper, salt and black pepper.

3. Add pasta, ½ cup reserved pasta water and butter; cook and stir until butter is melted and pasta is well coated. Stir in ½ cup Parmesan cheese. Serve immediately with additional cheese and basil.

LENTILS WITH PASTA

MAKES 6 TO 8 SERVINGS

- **1 cup dried lentils, rinsed and sorted**
- **1 cup dried split peas, rinsed and sorted**
- **1 tablespoon extra virgin olive oil**
- **1 onion, chopped**
- **2 tablespoons tomato paste**
- **2 cloves garlic, minced**
- **1 teaspoon salt**
- **¼ teaspoon black pepper**
- **3 cups water**
- **1 can (about 14 ounces) diced tomatoes**
- **12 ounces uncooked short pasta (elbow macaroni, small shells, ditalini or similar)**
- **Shredded Romano or Parmesan cheese (optional)**

1. Place lentils and split peas in medium bowl; cover with water. Let stand at least 10 minutes.

2. Heat oil in large saucepan or Dutch oven over medium heat. Add onion; cook and stir 5 minutes or until onion is lightly browned. Add tomato paste, garlic, salt and pepper; cook and stir 1 minute. Add 3 cups water and tomatoes; bring to a boil.

3. Drain lentils and split peas and add to saucepan. Reduce heat to medium-low; cover and simmer about 40 minutes or until lentils and split peas are tender.

4. Meanwhile, cook pasta in large saucepan of salted boiling water according to package directions for al dente. Drain and add to lentil mixture; mix well. Serve with cheese, if desired.

SPAGHETTI WITH BROWNED BUTTER AND MIZITHRA

MAKES 4 SERVINGS

- **1 package (16 ounces) uncooked spaghetti**
- **2 ounces Romano cheese, grated, plus additional for garnish**
- **2 ounces mizithra cheese, grated**
- **½ cup (1 stick) unsalted butter**
- **2 tablespoons finely chopped fresh parsley**

1 Cook pasta in large saucepan of salted boiling water according to package directions for al dente; drain and place in large bowl. Combine Romano and mizithra in small bowl; mix well.

2 Meanwhile, melt butter in small saucepan over medium heat. Continue cooking about 5 minutes or until butter turns deep golden brown and has a nutty aroma. (Watch carefully and swirl pan occasionally, as butter can turn from browned to burned quickly.)

3 Drizzle butter over pasta; sprinkle with cheese mixture and parsley and toss to coat. Serve immediately; garnish with additional Romano.

NOTE

Mizithra is a firm, salty, sheep or goat cheese from Greece. If mizithra is unavailable, substitute Parmesan, Asiago or additional Romano cheese.

ORZO WITH SPINACH AND RED PEPPER

MAKES 4 SERVINGS

- 4 ounces uncooked orzo pasta
- 2 tablespoons extra virgin olive oil
- 1 red bell pepper, diced
- 3 cloves garlic, minced
- 1 package (10 ounces) frozen chopped spinach, thawed and squeezed dry
- ¼ cup grated Parmesan cheese
- ½ teaspoon salt
- ½ teaspoon finely chopped fresh oregano or basil
- ¼ teaspoon lemon-pepper seasoning

1. Cook pasta in large saucepan of salted boiling water according to package directions for al dente. Drain and set aside.
2. Heat oil in large skillet over medium-high heat. Add bell pepper and garlic; cook and stir 2 to 3 minutes or until bell pepper is crisp-tender. Add orzo and spinach; cook and stir until heated through. Remove from heat.
3. Stir in cheese, salt, oregano, if desired, and lemon-pepper seasoning. Serve immediately.

PASTA WITH ONIONS AND GOAT CHEESE

MAKES 4 SERVINGS

- 2 tablespoons extra virgin olive oil
- 3 to 4 cups thinly sliced sweet onions
- ¾ cup (3 ounces) crumbled goat cheese
- ¼ cup milk
- 8 ounces uncooked campanelle or farfalle (bowtie) pasta
- 1 clove garlic, minced
- 2 tablespoons dry white wine or vegetable broth
- 1 tablespoons chopped fresh sage *or* 1 teaspoon dried sage
- ½ teaspoon salt
- ¼ teaspoon black pepper
- ¼ cup chopped walnuts

1. Heat oil in large skillet over medium heat. Add onions; cook 20 to 25 minutes or until golden brown, stirring occasionally.
2. Combine goat cheese and milk in small bowl; mash and stir until well blended and smooth.
3. Cook pasta in large saucepan of salted boiling water according to package directions for al dente. Drain and return to saucepan; keep warm.
4. Add garlic to caramelized onions in skillet; cook and stir about 3 minutes or until softened. Add wine, sage, salt and pepper; cook until liquid has evaporated. Remove from heat. Add pasta and goat cheese mixture; stir gently until cheese is melted and pasta is coated. Sprinkle with walnuts.

CREAMY LEMON LINGUINE

MAKES 2 TO 3 SERVINGS

- 8 ounces uncooked linguine
- 3 tablespoons fresh lemon juice
- 2 tablespoons butter
- 2 tablespoons minced fresh chives
- 2 tablespoons all-purpose flour
- ½ cup milk
- 1 tablespoon minced fresh dill *or* 1 teaspoon dried dill weed
- 1 tablespoon minced fresh parsley *or* 1 teaspoon dried parsley flakes
- 2 teaspoons grated lemon peel
- ½ teaspoon salt
- ¼ teaspoon ground white pepper
- 3 tablespoons grated Romano or Parmesan cheese

1 Cook linguine in large saucepan of salted boiling water according to package directions for al dente. Drain and place in medium bowl; sprinkle with lemon juice.

2 Melt butter in small saucepan over medium heat. Add chives; cook 2 to 3 minutes or until tender. Whisk in flour until well blended. Gradually whisk in milk until well blended; cook and stir until sauce is thickened. Stir in dill, parsley, lemon peel, salt and white pepper.

3 Pour sauce over linguine. Sprinkle with cheese; toss to coat evenly. Serve immediately.

SPAGHETTI AGLIO E OLIO

MAKES 4 SERVINGS

- 12 ounces uncooked spaghetti or thin spaghetti
- ⅓ cup plus 1 tablespoon extra virgin olive oil, divided
- 1 cup fresh Italian or French bread crumbs*
- 4 cloves garlic, very thinly sliced
- ¾ teaspoon salt
- ½ teaspoon red pepper flakes
- ½ cup chopped fresh parsley
- ¾ cup shredded Parmesan cheese, divided

**To make fresh bread crumbs, tear 2 ounces bread into pieces; process in food processor until coarse crumbs form.*

1. Cook spaghetti in large saucepan of salted boiling water according to package directions for al dente.

2. Meanwhile, heat 1 tablespoon oil in large skillet over medium heat. Add bread crumbs; cook 4 to 5 minutes or until golden brown, stirring frequently. Transfer to small bowl; set aside.

3. Add remaining ⅓ cup oil, garlic, salt and red pepper flakes to same skillet; cook about 3 minutes or until garlic just begins to brown on edges.

4. Drain pasta; reserve ½ cup pasta cooking water. Add pasta and parsley to skillet; toss to coat with oil mixture. Add some of reserved pasta water to moisten pasta, if desired. Stir in bread crumbs and ½ cup cheese. Top with remaining ¼ cup cheese before serving.

SPICED CHICKEN SKEWERS

MAKES 8 SERVINGS

- 1 cup plain Greek yogurt
- ¼ cup chopped fresh parsley, plus additional for garnish
- ¼ cup tahini
- 2 tablespoons fresh lemon juice
- 1 clove garlic
- ¾ teaspoon salt, divided
- 2 tablespoons extra virgin olive oil
- 2 teaspoons garam masala
- 1 pound boneless skinless chicken breasts, cut into 1-inch pieces

1 For sauce, combine yogurt, ¼ cup parsley, tahini, lemon juice, garlic and ¼ teaspoon salt in medium bowl; whisk until smooth.

2 Prepare grill for direct cooking. Spray grate with nonstick cooking spray.

3 Combine oil, garam masala and remaining ½ teaspoon salt in medium bowl. Add chicken; toss to coat. Thread chicken on eight 6-inch skewers.

4 Grill chicken over medium-high heat 5 minutes per side or until chicken is cooked through (165°F) and no longer pink in center. Serve with sauce. Garnish with additional parsley.

LEMON-GARLIC SALMON WITH TZATZIKI SAUCE

MAKES 4 SERVINGS

- **½ cup diced cucumber**
- **¾ teaspoon salt, divided**
- **1 cup plain Greek yogurt**
- **2 tablespoons fresh lemon juice, divided**
- **1 teaspoon grated lemon peel, divided**
- **1 teaspoon minced garlic, divided**
- **¼ teaspoon black pepper**
- **4 skinless salmon fillets (4 ounces each)**

1 Place cucumber in small colander set over small bowl; sprinkle with ¼ teaspoon salt. Drain 1 hour.

2 For tzatziki sauce, stir yogurt, cucumber, 1 tablespoon lemon juice, ½ teaspoon lemon peel, ½ teaspoon garlic and ¼ teaspoon salt in small bowl until combined. Cover and refrigerate until ready to use.

3 Combine remaining 1 tablespoon lemon juice, ½ teaspoon lemon peel, ½ teaspoon garlic, ¼ teaspoon salt and pepper in small bowl; mix well. Rub evenly over salmon.

4 Heat nonstick grill pan over medium-high heat. Add salmon; cook 5 minutes per side or until fish begins to flake when tested with fork. Serve with tzatziki sauce.

LAMB KEFTEDES WITH TANGY GREEK SALAD

MAKES 6 SERVINGS

LAMB KEFTEDES

- 3 slices multigrain bread, finely chopped
- ½ cup milk
- 1 cup finely diced onion
- 2 egg whites
- 1 tablespoon chopped fresh oregano
- 2 cloves garlic, minced
- ½ teaspoon salt
- 1 pound ground lamb

TANGY GREEK SALAD

- 1½ cups diced cucumber
- 1½ cups diced tomatoes
- Juice of 1 lemon
- 1 tablespoon extra virgin olive oil
- ¼ teaspoon salt
- ⅛ teaspoon black pepper

1. Line baking sheet with parchment paper. Combine bread cubes and milk in large bowl; toss to coat. Let stand 20 to 30 minutes or until liquid is absorbed and bread is fully soaked.
2. Add onion, eggs, oregano, garlic and ½ teaspoon salt to bread cubes; gently toss. Add lamb; mix well. Shape mixture into 36 (½-inch) balls. Place on prepared baking sheet. Refrigerate 30 minutes.
3. Meanwhile for salad, combine cucumber, tomatoes, lemon juice, oil, ¼ teaspoon salt and pepper in medium bowl; mix gently.
4. Preheat oven to 400°F. Place wire rack on large rimmed baking sheet. Transfer meatballs to rack.
5. Bake 20 minutes or until cooked through, turning once halfway through. Serve with salad.

SEAFOOD NIÇOISE

MAKES 4 SERVINGS

- 2 tablespoons extra virgin olive oil
- 1 leek, white part only, thinly sliced (1 cup)
- 2 shallots, finely chopped
- 6 to 8 small red potatoes, cut into quarters
- 1 can (15 ounces) tomato purée
- 1 to 1½ cups bottled clam juice, divided
- 1 teaspoon salt
- 1 teaspoon herbes de Provence*
- ¼ teaspoon dried tarragon leaves
- 1 pound sea scallops or tuna, cut into 1-inch pieces
- ½ cup sliced pitted black olives
- ½ cup frozen French-cut string beans (optional)

**Or substitute ¼ teaspoon each ground sage, dried rosemary, thyme, oregano, marjoram and basil.*

1. Heat oil in large saucepan or Dutch oven over medium-high heat. Add leek and shallots; cook and stir until soft. Add potatoes; cook 10 minutes, stirring occasionally.

2. Stir in tomato purée, 1 cup clam juice, salt and herbs; bring to a boil over high heat. Reduce heat to low; cover and simmer 40 minutes or until potatoes are fork-tender.

3. If sauce is too thick, add remaining ½ cup clam juice. Add scallops, olives and beans, if desired. Cover and simmer 5 to 6 minutes until scallops are opaque.

CHICKEN CASSOULET

MAKES 6 SERVINGS

- 4 slices bacon
- ¼ cup all-purpose flour
- 1¾ pounds bone-in chicken pieces
- Salt and black pepper
- 2 chicken sausages (2¼ ounces each), cooked and cut into ¼-inch pieces
- 1 medium onion, chopped
- 1½ cups diced red and green bell peppers
- 2 cloves garlic, minced
- 1 teaspoon dried thyme
- 1 teaspoon olive oil
- ½ cup dry white wine
- 2 cans (about 15 ounces each) cannellini or Great Northern beans, rinsed and drained

1. Preheat oven to 350°F.

2. Cook bacon in Dutch oven over medium-high heat until crisp; drain on paper towel-lined plate. Cut into 1-inch pieces. Reserve bacon drippings.

3. Place flour in shallow bowl. Season chicken all over with salt and pepper. Coat chicken with flour; shake off excess. Cook chicken in batches in reserved bacon drippings in Dutch oven over medium-high heat until browned; remove to plate. Add sausages to Dutch oven; cook and stir until lightly browned. Remove to plate with chicken.

4. Add onion, bell peppers, garlic and thyme to Dutch oven; cook and stir over medium heat 5 minutes or until vegetables are softened, adding oil as needed to prevent sticking. Add wine, stirring to scrape up browned bits. Add beans; mix well. Top with chicken, sausages and bacon.

5. Cover and bake 40 minutes. Uncover; bake 15 minutes or until chicken is cooked through (165°F).

TUNA SICILIAN STYLE

MAKES 4 SERVINGS

- ¾ cup extra virgin olive oil
- Juice of 2 lemons
- 4 cloves garlic, minced
- 1 tablespoon chopped fresh rosemary *or* 1½ teaspoons dried rosemary
- 1 tablespoon chopped fresh parsley
- ¾ teaspoon salt
- ½ teaspoon black pepper
- 4 fresh tuna steaks (½ inch thick)
- Lemon slices (optional)
- Arugula or spinach

1. For sauce, whisk oil, lemon juice, garlic, rosemary, parsley, salt and pepper in small bowl until well blended. Prepare grill for direct cooking.*

2. Set aside half of sauce until ready to serve. Brush both sides of tuna with sauce; place on grate over medium-high heat. Grill tuna 4 minutes, basting generously with sauce. Turn and grill 4 to 6 minutes, or until desired degree of doneness, brushing frequently with sauce. Add lemon slices to grill for last few minutes, if desired.

3. Transfer tuna to serving dish; keep warm. Heat reserved sauce in small saucepan over low heat. Arrange arugula around fish; drizzle with warmed sauce. Garnish with lemon slices.

**Tuna may also be prepared on stovetop grill pan.*

PORK CHOPS WITH VINEGAR PEPPERS ▸

MAKES 4 SERVINGS

- 4 pork rib chops (about 1 inch thick)
- ½ teaspoon salt
- ¼ teaspoon black pepper
- 2 tablespoons extra virgin olive oil
- 1½ cups seeded hot cherry peppers, cut into ½-inch slices*
- 2 cloves garlic, minced
- ¼ cup liquid from cherry pepper jar
- ¼ cup water
- 1 sprig fresh rosemary

**Hot cherry peppers are also available presliced in rings.*

1. Pat pork chops dry with paper towels. Season both sides of pork with salt and black pepper.
2. Heat oil in large skillet over medium-high heat. Add pork; cook about 5 minutes per side or until browned. Remove to plate; keep warm.
3. Add cherry peppers and garlic to skillet; cook and stir 2 minutes over medium heat, stirring to scrape up browned bits. Stir in cherry pepper liquid, water and rosemary.
4. Return pork to skillet; cover and cook about 6 minutes or until pork is barely pink in center.

SIMPLE COQ AU VIN

MAKES 4 SERVINGS

- 4 chicken leg quarters
- Salt and black pepper
- 2 tablespoons extra virgin olive oil
- 8 ounces mushrooms, sliced
- 1 onion, cut into rings
- ½ cup dry red wine
- ½ teaspoon dried basil
- ½ teaspoon dried thyme
- ½ teaspoon dried oregano

SLOW COOKER DIRECTIONS

1. Season chicken all over with salt and pepper. Heat oil in large skillet over medium-high heat. Add chicken; brown on all sides. Transfer chicken to slow cooker.
2. Heat same skillet over medium heat. Add mushrooms and onion; cook and stir 5 minutes or until tender. Add wine, stirring to scrape up browned bits. Pour over chicken in slow cooker. Sprinkle with basil, thyme and oregano. Cover; cook on LOW 8 to 10 hours or on HIGH 3 to 4 hours.

SEAFOOD GRATIN ▸

MAKES 6 SERVINGS

- 8 ounces cooked shrimp
- 8 ounces cooked crabmeat
- 8 ounces cooked sole
- 8 ounces cooked lobster
- 2 tablespoons butter
- 2 tablespoons all-purpose flour
- 1 cup milk
- ¾ cup grated Parmesan cheese
- Salt and black pepper
- Panko bread crumbs

1 Preheat oven to 325°F. Grease 2-quart baking dish or 6 individual baking dishes. Cut seafood into bite-sized pieces; place in prepared baking dish.

2 Melt butter in small saucepan over medium heat. Whisk in flour until well blended. Whisk in milk in thin steady stream; cook until thickened, stirring constantly. Stir in cheese. Season to taste with salt and pepper. Pour sauce over seafood; top with bread crumbs.

3 Bake gratin 20 to 25 minutes. Cool slightly before serving.

GREEK LEMON CHICKEN

MAKES 4 SERVINGS

- 4 boneless skinless chicken breasts (6 to 8 ounces each)
- 2 tablespoons fresh lemon juice
- 3 tablespoons extra virgin olive oil, divided
- 1 teaspoon grated lemon peel
- 1 teaspoon dried oregano
- 1 clove garlic, minced
- ½ teaspoon salt
- ⅛ teaspoon black pepper

1 Place chicken in large resealable food storage bag. Add lemon juice, 1 tablespoon oil, lemon peel, oregano, garlic, salt and pepper. Seal bag; shake to coat chicken. Marinate in refrigerator at least 30 minutes or up to 8 hours, turning occasionally.

2 Remove chicken from marinade; discard marinade. Heat remaining 2 tablespoons oil in large nonstick skillet over medium heat. Add chicken; cook 3 minutes. Turn chicken. Reduce heat to medium-low; cook 10 minutes or until cooked through (165°F) and no longer pink in center.

GREEK LAMB WITH TZATZIKI SAUCE

MAKES 4 SERVINGS

- **2½ to 3 pounds boneless leg of lamb**
- **8 cloves garlic, divided**
- **¼ cup Dijon mustard**
- **2 tablespoons minced fresh rosemary leaves**
- **2 teaspoons salt**
- **2 teaspoons black pepper**
- **¼ cup plus 2 teaspoons extra virgin olive oil, divided**
- **1 seedless cucumber**
- **1 tablespoon chopped fresh mint**
- **1 teaspoon fresh lemon juice**
- **2 cups plain Greek yogurt, labneh or sour cream**

1. Untie and unroll lamb to lie flat; trim fat.
2. For marinade, mince 4 cloves garlic; place in small bowl. Add mustard, rosemary, salt and pepper; whisk in ¼ cup oil. Spread mixture evenly over lamb, coating both sides. Place lamb in large resealable food storage bag. Seal bag; refrigerate at least 2 hours or overnight, turning several times.
3. Meanwhile for tzatziki sauce, mince remaining 4 cloves garlic and mash to a paste; place in medium bowl. Peel and grate cucumber; squeeze to remove excess moisture. Add cucumber, mint, remaining 2 teaspoons oil and lemon juice to bowl with garlic. Add yogurt; mix well. Refrigerate until ready to serve.
4. Prepare grill for direct cooking. Grill lamb over medium-high heat 35 to 40 minutes or to desired doneness. Cover loosely with foil; let rest 5 to 10 minutes. (Remove from grill at 140°F for medium. Temperature will rise 5°F while resting.)
5. Slice lamb and serve with tzatziki sauce.

TUSCAN PORK LOIN ROAST WITH FIG SAUCE ▸

MAKES 6 TO 8 SERVINGS

- 2 tablespoons extra virgin olive oil
- 3 cloves garlic, minced
- 2 teaspoons salt
- 2 teaspoons dried rosemary
- ½ teaspoon red pepper flakes *or* 1 teaspoon black pepper
- 1 center cut boneless pork loin roast (about 3 pounds)
- ¼ cup dry red wine
- 1 jar (about 8 ounces) fig jam

1. Preheat oven to 350°F. Combine oil, garlic, salt, rosemary and red pepper flakes in small bowl; brush over roast. Place pork on rack in shallow roasting pan.
2. Roast 1 hour or until internal temperature is 145°F. Transfer to cutting board. Tent with foil; let stand 10 minutes.
3. Meanwhile, pour wine into roasting pan; cook over medium-high heat 2 minutes, stirring to scrape up browned bits. Stir in fig jam; cook and stir until heated through. Slice pork; serve with sauce.

GREEK-STYLE BRAISED LAMB CHOPS

MAKES 4 SERVINGS

- 1 teaspoon Greek seasoning
- 4 lamb shoulder chops (about 2½ pounds)
- 3 tablespoons extra virgin olive oil
- 1 onion, halved and sliced
- 1 bottle (12 ounces) beer
- 3 plum tomatoes, each cut into 6 wedges
- ½ cup pitted Kalamata olives

1. Rub Greek seasoning all over lamb.
2. Heat oil in large skillet over medium-high heat. Working in batches, brown lamb on all sides. Remove to large plate. Add onion to skillet; cook and stir 3 to 5 minutes or until softened. Pour in beer. Bring to a boil over high heat, stirring to scrape up browned bits. Reduce heat to low; add lamb, tomatoes and olives. Cover and simmer 1 hour or until meat is tender.
3. Remove lamb and vegetables to serving platter using slotted spoon. Tent with foil to keep warm. Bring remaining liquid to a boil over high heat; cook until reduced to 1 cup. Serve lamb and vegetables with sauce.

TUNA STEAKS WITH TOMATOES AND OLIVES

MAKES 4 SERVINGS

- 2 tablespoons extra virgin olive oil, divided
- 1 onion, quartered and sliced
- 1 clove garlic, minced
- 1½ cups chopped seeded tomatoes
- ¼ cup sliced pitted black olives
- 2 anchovy fillets, finely chopped (optional)
- 2 tablespoons chopped fresh basil
- ¾ teaspoon salt, divided
- ⅛ teaspoon red pepper flakes
- 4 tuna steaks (¾ inch thick)
- Black pepper
- ¼ cup toasted pine nuts*

**To toast pine nuts, cook in medium skillet over medium heat 3 to 4 minutes or until lightly browned and fragrant, stirring frequently.*

1 Heat 1 tablespoon oil in large skillet over medium heat. Add onion; cook and stir 5 minutes or until softened. Add garlic; cook and stir 30 seconds. Add tomatoes; cook 3 minutes, stirring occasionally. Stir in olives, anchovies, if desired, basil, ¼ teaspoon salt and red pepper flakes; cook until most of liquid has evaporated.

2 Sprinkle tuna with remaining ½ teaspoon salt and black pepper. Heat remaining 1 tablespoon oil in large nonstick skillet over medium-high heat. Add tuna; cook 2 minutes per side or until medium rare. Serve with tomato mixture; sprinkle with pine nuts.

SWORDFISH POMODORO

MAKES 6 SERVINGS

- 1½ pounds swordfish steaks (¾ inch thick)
- Salt and black pepper
- 2 tablespoons all-purpose flour
- 3 tablespoons extra virgin olive oil, divided
- 1 medium onion, halved and thinly sliced
- 1 clove garlic, minced
- 1½ cups chopped seeded tomatoes
- ⅓ cup drained mild giardiniera*
- 2 tablespoons dry white wine (optional)
- 1 tablespoon chopped fresh oregano *or* 1 teaspoon dried oregano

**Giardiniera is an Italian term for pickled vegetables. Available mild or hot, giardiniera can be found in the pickle or ethnic foods section of the supermarket.*

1. Season fish with salt and pepper. Place flour in shallow dish; coat fish with flour.

2. Heat 1 tablespoon oil in medium skillet over medium heat. Add onion; cook and stir 5 minutes or until softened. Add garlic; cook and stir 30 seconds. Add tomatoes; cook 3 minutes, stirring occasionally. Stir in giardiniera, wine, if desired, and oregano. Cook 3 minutes or until most liquid is evaporated.

3. Heat remaining 2 tablespoons oil in large nonstick skillet over medium-high heat. Add fish; cook 4 minutes per side or until fish begins to flake when tested with fork. Serve tomato mixture over fish.

MOUSSAKA

MAKES 6 TO 8 SERVINGS

- **1 large eggplant, cut lengthwise into ½-inch-thick slices**
- **2½ teaspoons salt, divided**
- **½ cup extra virgin olive oil, divided**
- **2 large russet potatoes, peeled and cut lengthwise into ¼-inch-thick slices**
- **2 large zucchini, cut lengthwise into ⅜-inch-thick slices**
- **1½ pounds ground beef or lamb**
- **1 large onion, chopped**
- **2 cloves garlic, minced**
- **1 cup chopped fresh tomatoes**
- **½ cup dry red or white wine**
- **¼ cup chopped fresh parsley**
- **¼ teaspoon ground cinnamon**
- **⅛ teaspoon black pepper**
- **1 cup grated Parmesan cheese, divided**
- **¼ cup (½ stick) butter**
- **⅓ cup all-purpose flour**
- **¼ teaspoon ground nutmeg**
- **2 cups milk**

1. Place eggplant in large colander; sprinkle with 1 teaspoon salt. Drain 30 minutes.
2. Heat ¼ cup oil in large skillet over medium heat. Add potatoes in single layer; cook 5 minutes per side or until tender and lightly browned. Remove potatoes from skillet; drain on paper towels. Add 2 tablespoons oil to skillet. Add zucchini; cook 2 minutes per side or until tender. Drain on paper towels. Add remaining 2 tablespoons oil to skillet. Add eggplant; cook 5 minutes per side or until tender. Drain on paper towels. Wipe out skillet with paper towels.
3. Heat same skillet over medium-high heat. Add beef, onion and garlic; cook and stir 5 minutes or until meat is no longer pink. Drain fat. Stir in tomatoes, wine, parsley, 1 teaspoon salt, cinnamon and pepper. Bring to a boil over high heat. Reduce heat to low. Simmer 10 minutes or until liquid is evaporated.
4. Preheat oven to 325°F. Grease 13×9-inch baking dish. Arrange potatoes in bottom; sprinkle with ¼ cup cheese. Top with zucchini and ¼ cup cheese, then eggplant and ¼ cup cheese. Spoon meat mixture over top.
5. For sauce, melt butter in medium saucepan over low heat. Whisk in flour, remaining ½ teaspoon salt and nutmeg. Cook 1 minute, whisking constantly. Gradually whisk in milk. Cook over medium heat, until mixture boils and thickens, whisking constantly. Pour sauce evenly over meat mixture in dish; sprinkle with remaining ¼ cup cheese. Bake 30 to 40 minutes or until hot and bubbly.

SHEET PAN MEDITERRANEAN CHICKEN

MAKES 6 SERVINGS

- ¼ cup extra virgin olive oil
- 4 cloves garlic, thinly sliced
- 1 tablespoon red wine vinegar
- 2 teaspoons salt
- 1½ teaspoons smoked paprika
- 1 teaspoon dried oregano
- ½ teaspoon black pepper
- 6 boneless skinless chicken thighs (about 2 pounds)
- 2 cans (about 15 ounces each) chickpeas, rinsed and drained
- 3 pints grape tomatoes
- ½ cup pitted Kalamata olives, cut into halves
- ¾ cup crumbled feta cheese
- ½ cup chopped fresh Italian parsley
- Hot cooked orzo

1. Preheat oven to 425°F. Line baking sheet with foil or spray with nonstick cooking spray.
2. Whisk oil, garlic, vinegar, salt, paprika, oregano and pepper in large bowl until well blended. Add chicken, chickpeas, tomatoes and olives; stir to coat well. Spread mixture on prepared baking sheet. (Baking sheet will be very full.)
3. Bake 18 to 20 minutes or until chicken is cooked through (165°F) and tomatoes are beginning to burst. *Turn oven to broil;* broil 2 to 3 minutes or until chicken begins to brown.
4. Sprinkle with cheese and parsley. Serve with hot cooked orzo.

GREEK-STYLE MEATBALLS AND SPINACH

MAKES 4 SERVINGS

- ½ cup old-fashioned oats
- ¼ cup minced onion
- 1 clove garlic, minced
- ½ teaspoon salt
- ¼ teaspoon dried oregano
- ⅛ teaspoon black pepper
- 8 ounces ground lamb
- 1 egg
- 1 cup beef broth
- ½ cup plain yogurt
- 1 teaspoon all-purpose flour
- 4 cups baby spinach, coarsely chopped
- 4 cups hot cooked egg noodles

SLOW COOKER DIRECTIONS

1 Combine oats, onion, garlic, salt, oregano and pepper in medium bowl. Add lamb and egg; mix gently until blended. Shape lamb mixture into 16 balls. Place in slow cooker. Add broth.

2 Cover and cook on LOW 6 hours.

3 Stir together yogurt and flour in small bowl. Spoon about ¼ cup hot liquid from slow cooker into yogurt. Stir until smooth. Stir yogurt mixture into liquid in slow cooker. Add spinach.

4 Cover; cook on LOW 10 minutes or until spinach is hot and whiled. Serve meatballs, spinach and sauce over noodles.

EGGS

SPANISH POTATO OMELET

MAKES 4 SERVINGS

- ¼ cup extra virgin olive oil
- ¼ cup vegetable oil
- 1 pound unpeeled red or white potatoes, cut into ⅛-inch slices
- ½ teaspoon salt, divided
- 1 small onion, cut in half lengthwise and thinly sliced crosswise
- ¼ cup chopped green bell pepper
- ¼ cup chopped red bell pepper
- 3 eggs

1. Heat oils in large skillet over medium-high heat. Add potatoes; turn several times to coat slices with oil. Sprinkle with ¼ teaspoon salt. Cook 6 to 9 minutes or until potatoes are translucent, turning occasionally. Add onion and peppers. Reduce heat to medium. Cook 10 minutes or until potatoes are tender, turning occasionally. Drain mixture in colander placed in large bowl; reserve oil. Let stand until cool.

2. Beat eggs with remaining ¼ teaspoon salt in another large bowl. Gently stir in potato mixture until covered with eggs. Let stand 15 minutes.

3. Heat 2 teaspoons reserved oil in small nonstick skillet over medium-high heat. Spread potato mixture in skillet to form solid layer. Cook until egg mixture on bottom and side of pan is set but top still looks moist. Cover skillet with plate. Flip omelet onto plate, then slide back into pan. Continue to cook until bottom is lightly browned. Slide omelet onto serving plate. Let stand 30 minutes before serving. Cut into wedges.

SPINACH, MUSHROOM, EGG AND GRUYÈRE ROLL-UPS

MAKES 4 SERVINGS

- **1 tablespoon plus 4 teaspoons extra virgin olive oil, divided**
- **1 shallot, thinly sliced (about ½ cup)**
- **1 package (6 ounces) fresh baby spinach**
- **1 clove garlic, minced**
- **½ teaspoon plus ⅛ teaspoon salt, divided**
- **8 ounces cremini mushrooms, thinly sliced**
- **¼ teaspoon black pepper, divided**
- **2 pieces flatbread, 9½×11-inches, lightly toasted**
- **⅔ cup shredded Grùyere cheese**
- **6 eggs**
- **2 tablespoons milk**
- **2 teaspoons Dijon mustard**

1. Heat 2 teaspoons oil in large nonstick skillet over medium heat. Add shallot; cook and stir 5 to 6 minutes or until softened. Add spinach; cook over medium-high heat 2 minutes or until wilted. Add garlic and ¼ teaspoon salt; cook and stir 1 minute. Transfer to small bowl.
2. Heat 1 tablespoon oil in same skillet over medium-high heat. Add mushrooms, ¼ teaspoon salt and ⅛ teaspoon pepper; cook 6 minutes or until browned, stirring occasionally.
3. Spread half of spinach-mushroom mixture on each flatbread; top with cheese.
4. Whisk eggs in large bowl. Add remaining ⅛ teaspoon salt, ⅛ teaspoon pepper, milk and mustard; whisk until blended.
5. Heat remaining 2 teaspoons oil in same skillet over medium-high heat. Add egg mixture; cook about 1 minute or until eggs are set but not dry, stirring frequently.
6. Spread cooked eggs over spinach; roll up flatbread. Cut rolls in half diagonally to serve.

ROASTED TOMATO QUICHE

MAKES 6 SERVINGS

- **1 pint grape tomatoes**
- **1 tablespoon olive oil**
- **Salt and black pepper**
- **2½ cups riced cauliflower (fresh or frozen)**
- **½ cup shredded Parmesan cheese**
- **6 eggs, divided**
- **½ teaspoon salt, divided**
- **½ teaspoon black pepper, divided**
- **¾ cup milk**
- **½ cup (2 ounces) shredded mozzarella cheese**
- **2 cloves garlic, minced**
- **½ teaspoon fresh thyme leaves**

1. Preheat oven to 350°F. Place tomatoes in shallow baking dish; drizzle with oil and sprinkle lightly with salt and pepper. Bake 1 hour, stirring once or twice.*

2. Spray 9-inch pie plate with nonstick cooking spray. Place cauliflower in large microwavable bowl; cover with plastic wrap and cut slit to vent. Microwave on HIGH 4 minutes; stir. Cover and cook on HIGH 4 minutes. Remove cover; cool slightly. Place cauliflower on double layer of paper towels; fold over paper towels and squeeze to remove excess moisture. Return to bowl. Add Parmesan cheese, 1 egg, ½ teaspoon salt and ¼ teaspoon pepper; mix well. Press onto bottom and up side of prepared pie plate. *Increase oven temperature to 425°F.* Bake crust 15 minutes. Remove from oven; place on sheet pan.

3. *Reduce oven temperature to 375°F.* Whisk 5 eggs, milk, mozzarella cheese, garlic, thyme, ¼ teaspoon salt and ¼ teaspoon black pepper in medium bowl until well blended. Place tomatoes in crust; pour egg mixture over tomatoes. Bake 45 minutes or until thin knife inserted into center comes out clean (a little cheese is okay). Cool 10 minutes before slicing.

**Tomatoes can be roasted a day in advance.*

NOTE

To make riced cauliflower, cut 1 head of cauliflower into 1-inch florets. Working in batches, pulse the florets in food processor until they form small rice-size pieces. If there are any large chunks left behind, pick them out and add them to your next batch. Or grate a whole head of cauliflower on the large holes of a box grater into a large bowl, rotating until all the florets are shredded.

FETA FRIED EGG ▸

MAKES 1 SERVING

- 2 tablespoons crumbled feta cheese
- 1 egg
- 1 tablespoon harissa sauce
- 1 pita bread or small naan bread, toasted

1 Heat small nonstick skillet over medium heat. Place feta in center of skillet; crack egg onto feta. Cook 2 minutes or until egg white is opaque. Cover skillet and cook until yolk is desired doneness. Remove cover; let any water cook off.

2 Spread harissa over pita; carefully transfer egg and feta to pita.

SPINACH QUICHE

MAKES 6 SERVINGS

- 1 tablespoon extra virgin olive oil
- 1 small onion, chopped
- 2 cloves garlic, minced
- 5 cups fresh spinach, stemmed and coarsely chopped
- ¾ teaspoon salt, divided
- 4 eggs
- ½ cup milk
- ⅓ cup semolina*
- ½ teaspoon black pepper
- 1¼ cups (5 ounces) shredded Cheddar Jack or Colby Jack cheese

**If semolina is not available, substitute fine ground cornmeal. Or substitute ⅓ cup of a cooked grain such as quinoa or rice.*

1 Preheat oven to 375°F. Spray 9-inch pie plate with nonstick cooking spray.

2 Heat oil in large skillet over medium heat. Add onion; cook and stir 5 minutes or until softened. Add garlic; cook and stir 1 minute. Add spinach and ¼ teaspoon salt; cook and stir about 4 minutes or until wilted. Remove from heat; set aside to cool slightly.

3 Whisk eggs, milk, semolina, remaining ½ teaspoon salt and pepper in large bowl until well blended. Stir in spinach mixture and cheese; mix well. Pour into prepared pie plate.

4 Bake 28 to 30 minutes or until center is set. Remove to wire rack; cool 10 minutes before serving.

SPANISH TORTILLA

MAKES 10 TO 12 SERVINGS

- **2 tablespoons extra virgin olive oil**
- **1 cup thinly sliced peeled potato**
- **1 small zucchini, thinly sliced**
- **¼ cup chopped onion**
- **1 clove garlic, minced**
- **1 teaspoon salt, divided**
- **1 cup shredded cooked chicken**
- **8 eggs**
- **½ teaspoon black pepper**
- **¼ teaspoon red pepper flakes**

1. Heat oil in 10-inch nonstick skillet over medium-high heat. Add potato, zucchini, onion, garlic and ½ teaspoon salt; cook and stir 5 minutes or until potato is tender, stirring frequently. Add chicken; cook and stir 1 minute.

2. Meanwhile, whisk eggs, remaining ½ teaspoon salt, black pepper and red pepper flakes in large bowl. Carefully pour egg mixture into skillet. Reduce heat to low; cover and cook 12 to 15 minutes or until set in center.

3. Loosen edges of tortilla; slide onto serving platter. Let stand 5 minutes before cutting into wedges.

GREEK ISLES OMELET

MAKES 2 SERVINGS

- **2 tablespoons extra virgin olive oil, divided**
- **¼ cup chopped onion**
- **¼ cup canned artichoke hearts, rinsed, drained and sliced**
- **½ cup chopped fresh spinach**
- **¼ cup chopped plum tomato**
- **2 tablespoons sliced pitted black olives, rinsed and drained**
- **4 eggs**
- **Salt and black pepper**

1. Heat 1 tablespoon oil in small nonstick skillet over medium heat. Add onion; cook and stir 2 minutes or until crisp-tender. Add artichokes; cook and stir until heated through. Stir in spinach, tomato and olives; cook 1 minute. Transfer to small bowl.

2. Whisk eggs in medium bowl until well blended; season with salt and pepper. Heat remaining 1 tablespoon oil in same skillet. Pour egg mixture into skillet; cook until just set, lifting edge to allow uncooked portion to flow underneath.

3. Spoon vegetable mixture over half of omelet. Gently loosen omelet with spatula and fold in half. Cut in half; serve immediately.

SPAGHETTI AND VEGETABLE FRITTATA

MAKES 6 SERVINGS

- **4 tablespoons extra virgin olive oil, divided**
- **1 package (8 ounces) sliced mushrooms**
- **1 cup thinly sliced leeks (white and light green parts)**
- **6 eggs**
- **⅓ cup milk**
- **3 tablespoons grated Parmesan cheese**
- **½ teaspoon salt**
- **⅛ teaspoon ground nutmeg**
- **⅛ teaspoon black pepper**
- **1 package (10 ounces) frozen chopped collard greens or spinach, thawed and squeezed dry**
- **2 cups cooked whole grain spaghetti**
- **½ cup (2 ounces) shredded mozzarella cheese**

1. Heat 2 tablespoons oil in large ovenproof skillet over medium-high heat. Add mushrooms and leeks; cook and stir 8 minutes or until lightly browned.
2. Whisk eggs, milk, Parmesan cheese, salt, nutmeg and pepper in large bowl. Stir in collard greens, spaghetti and mushroom mixture. Heat remaining 2 tablespoons oil in same skillet over medium-low heat. Add egg mixture; cover and cook 10 minutes or until top is set.
3. Meanwhile, preheat broiler. Sprinkle mozzarella cheese over frittata; broil about 5 inches from heat 3 minutes or until golden brown. Cut into wedges.

TIP

Turn tonight's dinner into tomorrow's breakfast or lunch. Cook more spaghetti than you need, measure 2 cups and place it in a food storage container. Stir in a bit of olive oil to prevent sticking and refrigerate until needed.

FRENCH CARROT QUICHE

MAKES 4 SERVINGS

- 1 tablespoon butter
- 1 pound carrots, peeled and sliced into rounds
- ¼ cup chopped green onions
- ½ teaspoon herbes de Provence
- 1 cup milk
- ¼ cup whipping cream
- ½ cup all-purpose flour
- 2 eggs
- ½ teaspoon minced fresh thyme
- ¼ teaspoon ground nutmeg
- ¼ teaspoon salt
- ½ cup (1 ounce) shredded Gruyère or Swiss cheese

1. Preheat oven to 350°F. Grease four shallow 1-cup baking dishes or one 9-inch quiche dish or shallow casserole.

2. Melt butter in large skillet over medium heat. Add carrots, green onions and herbes de Provence; cook and stir 5 to 7 minutes or until carrots are tender.

3. Meanwhile, combine milk and cream in medium bowl; gradually whisk in flour. Whisk in eggs, thyme, nutmeg and salt.

4. Spread carrot mixture in prepared dishes; top evenly with milk mixture. Sprinkle with cheese. Bake 20 to 25 minutes for individual quiches (or 30 to 40 minutes for 9-inch quiche) or until firm. Serve warm or at room temperature.

BROCCOLI FRITTATA

MAKES 6 SERVINGS

- 1 broccoli crown
- 2 tablespoons olive oil
- 1 small red bell pepper, finely chopped
- 4 green onions, chopped
- 2 cloves garlic, minced
- 1 teaspoon smoked paprika
- ¾ teaspoon salt, divided
- 8 eggs
- ¼ cup milk
- ¼ cup grated Parmesan cheese
- ¼ teaspoon black pepper
- ¾ cup crumbled feta cheese

1. Preheat oven to 350°F. Peel off tough outer skin of broccoli stem with paring knife; chop stem into ¼-inch pieces. Cut top of broccoli into ½-inch florets.

2. Heat oil in large (10-inch) ovenproof nonstick skillet over medium-high heat. Add broccoli, cook 7 minutes, stirring occasionally. Add bell pepper, green onions, garlic, paprika and ¼ teaspoon salt; cook and stir 3 minutes or until bell pepper is softened.

3. Beat eggs, milk, Parmesan cheese, remaining ½ teaspoon salt and black pepper in medium bowl until well blended. Pour over vegetables in skillet; stir gently to make sure vegetables are spread out in skillet and egg mixture is evenly distributed. Cook about 2 minutes or until edges begin to set. Sprinkle with feta cheese.

4. Transfer skillet to oven; bake about 20 minutes or just until eggs are set. Cool at least 5 minutes; cut into wedges. Serve warm or at room temperature.

GOAT CHEESE, CARAMELIZED ONION AND PROSCIUTTO FLATBREAD BITES

MAKES 6 SERVINGS

- 2 tablespoons extra virgin olive oil, plus additional for drizzling
- 1 large onion, sliced
- ¼ teaspoon salt
- ¼ cup water
- 1 package (about 14 ounces) refrigerated pizza dough
- 2 ounces goat cheese, crumbled
- 4 slices prosciutto
- ½ teaspoon fresh thyme leaves

1. Preheat oven to 450°F. Line baking sheet with parchment paper.
2. Heat 2 tablespoons oil in large skillet over medium heat. Add onion and salt; cook 18 to 20 minutes or until onion is deep golden brown, stirring occasionally and adding water halfway through cooking. Cool slightly.
3. Roll out dough into two 9×5-inch rectangles on lightly floured surface. Transfer dough to prepared baking sheet; top with onion, goat cheese and prosciutto.
4. Bake 12 minutes or until crust is golden brown and prosciutto is crisp. Drizzle with additional oil and sprinkle with thyme. Cut into strips to serve.

OPEN-FACED LAMB NAAN SANDWICHES

MAKES 4 SERVINGS

- **1 tablespoon extra virgin olive oil**
- **1 red onion, chopped**
- **1 pound ground lamb**
- **1 tablespoon tomato paste**
- **1¼ teaspoons salt, divided**
- **1¼ teaspoons minced garlic, divided**
- **1 teaspoon ground cumin**
- **½ teaspoon ground corinader**
- **¾ cup plain Greek yogurt**
- **¼ cup diced cucumber**
- **2 tablespoons chopped fresh cilantro**
- **4 pieces naan bread, lightly toasted**

1. Heat oil in large skillet over medium heat. Add onion; cook and stir about 8 to 10 minutes or until softened. Transfer to small bowl.

2. Heat same skillet over medium-high heat. Add lamb; cook about 8 minutes or until browned, stirring to break up meat. Add tomato paste, 1 teaspoon salt, 1 teaspoon garlic, cumin and coriander; cook 1 minute, stirring constantly. Add onion; cook 1 minute.

3. Combine yogurt, cucumber, cilantro, remaining ¼ teaspoon garlic and ¼ teaspoon salt in medium bowl; mix well.

4. Divide lamb evenly among warmed naan; top with yogurt mixture. Serve immediately.

TUSCAN PORTOBELLO MELT

MAKES 2 SERVINGS

- 1 portobello mushroom cap, thinly sliced
- ½ small red onion, thinly sliced
- ½ cup grape tomatoes
- 1 tablespoon extra virgin olive oil
- 1 teaspoon balsamic vinegar
- ⅛ teaspoon salt
- ⅛ teaspoon dried thyme
- ⅛ teaspoon black pepper
- 2 tablespoons butter, softened, divided
- 4 slices sourdough bread
- 2 slices provolone cheese
- 2 teaspoons Dijon mustard
- 2 slices Monterey Jack cheese

1. Preheat broiler. Combine mushroom, onion and tomatoes in small baking pan. Drizzle with oil and vinegar; sprinkle with salt, thyme and pepper. Toss to coat. Spread vegetables in single layer in pan.
2. Broil 6 minutes or until vegetables are softened and browned, stirring once.
3. Heat medium skillet over medium heat. Spread half of butter over one side of each bread slice. Place buttered side down in skillet; cook 2 minutes or until bread is toasted. Transfer bread to cutting board, toasted sides up.
4. Place provolone cheese on two bread slices; spread mustard over cheese. Top with vegetables, Monterey Jack cheese and remaining bread slices, toasted sides down. Spread remaining half of butter over outside of sandwiches.
5. Cook in same skillet over medium heat 5 minutes or until bread is toasted and cheese is melted, turning once.

KHACHAPURI (GEORGIAN CHEESE BREAD)

MAKES 2 SERVINGS

- 1 loaf (16 ounces) frozen bread dough, thawed according to package directions
- 1½ cups (6 ounces) shredded mozzarella cheese
- 1½ cups (6 ounces) crumbled feta cheese
- 1 teaspoon olive oil
- 1 teaspoon everything bagel seasoning (optional)
- 2 eggs
- Black pepper

1. Line baking sheet with parchment paper. Divide dough in half. Roll out one half into 11×8½-inch oval on lightly floured surface; place on prepared baking sheet.

2. Combine mozzarella cheese and feta cheese in medium bowl; mix well. Sprinkle ½ cup cheese mixture over dough, spreading almost to edge. Starting with long sides of oval, roll up dough and cheese towards center, curving into boat shape and leaving about 3 inches open in center. Press ends to seal. Fill center with 1 cup cheese mixture. Repeat rolling and filling steps with remaining half of dough and cheese mixture.

3. Cover loosely with plastic wrap; let rise 20 to 30 minutes or until puffy. Preheat oven to 400°F. Just before baking, brush edges of dough with oil; sprinkle with everything bagel seasoning, if desired.

4. Bake 12 minutes. Remove baking sheet from oven; use back of spoon to create indentations for eggs in center of cheese. Crack egg into each indentation;* sprinkle with pepper.

5. Bake 8 minutes for soft eggs; bake 10 minutes for firm eggs.

**For more control, crack egg into small bowl and slide egg from bowl into cheese mixture.*

ZUCCHINI PIZZA

MAKES 4 SERVINGS

- 4 tablespoons extra virgin olive oil, divided
- 1 large sweet onion, halved and thinly sliced
- 2 medium zucchini, grated
- ¾ teaspoon salt, divided
- ¼ teaspoon garlic powder
- ¼ teaspoon black pepper
- 1 package (16 ounces) refrigerated pizza dough (do not use canned)
- 1⅓ cups shredded pizza blend cheese, divided
- 2 tablespoons chopped fresh parsley
- Red pepper flakes (optional)

1. Heat 1 tablespoon oil in medium skillet over medium heat. Add onion; cook 35 to 40 minutes or until deep golden brown, stirring occasionally and adding water by tablespoonfuls if onion is dry. Stir in ¼ teaspoon salt; set aside to cool.

2. Meanwhile for zucchini butter, squeeze excess liquid from zucchini. Heat 1 tablespoon oil in large skillet over medium-high heat. Add zucchini, ½ teaspoon salt and garlic powder; cook and stir 5 minutes or until zucchini begins to soften. Reduce heat to medium; cook about 30 minutes or until zucchini is very soft. Stir in pepper; set aside to cool.

3. Preheat oven to 450°F. Line baking sheet with parchment paper. Roll out dough into 12-inch circle on lightly floured surface. (If dough is too difficult to roll, cover and let stand 20 minutes.) Transfer dough to prepared baking sheet.

4. Brush entire surface of dough, including edge, with remaining 2 tablespoons oil. Sprinkle with ⅔ cup cheese; top with caramelized onion and zucchini butter. Sprinkle with remaining ⅔ cup cheese.

5. Bake about 12 minutes or until crust is golden brown. Sprinkle with parsley and red pepper flakes, if desired. Cut into wedges to serve.

FOCACCIA

MAKES 12 SERVINGS

- 1½ cups warm water (105° to 115°F)
- 1 package (¼ ounce) active dry yeast
- 1 teaspoon sugar
- 4 cups all-purpose flour
- 9 tablespoons extra virgin olive oil, divided
- 2 teaspoons salt
- 1 teaspoon flaky or kosher salt

1. Combine water, yeast and sugar in large bowl of stand mixer; stir to dissolve yeast. Let stand 5 minutes or until mixture is bubbly. Add flour, 3 tablespoons oil and salt; stir to form dough. Attach dough hook to mixer; knead at low speed 5 minutes or until dough is smooth and elastic.* Place dough in large greased bowl; turn to grease top. Cover and let rise in warm place 1 hour or until doubled in size.

2. Place 3 tablespoons oil in 13×9-inch baking pan. Turn out dough into pan; spread gently to edges of pan. If dough will not stretch, let rest 10 minutes. Dimple dough all over with fingers. Cover and let rise in warm place 30 minutes or until doubled in size.

3. Preheat oven to 400°F. Brush remaining 3 tablespoons oil over top of dough; sprinkle with flaky salt, if desired. Bake 15 to 20 minutes or until top is firm and golden brown. Cool slightly in pan. Remove to cutting board; cut into squares or strips to serve.

**Or knead on lightly floured surface. Fold dough in half toward you and press dough away from you with heels of hands. Give dough a quarter turn and continue folding, pushing and turning. Continue kneading 5 minutes or until dough is smooth and elastic.*

MOZZARELLA IN CARROZZA

MAKES 4 TO 8 SERVINGS

- 2 eggs
- ⅓ cup milk
- ¼ teaspoon salt
- ⅛ teaspoon black pepper
- 8 slices country Italian bread
- 8 to 12 fresh basil leaves, torn
- 8 oil-packed sun-dried tomatoes, drained and cut into strips
- 8 ounces fresh mozzarella, cut into ¼-inch slices
- 1½ tablespoons extra virgin olive oil

1. Whisk eggs, milk, salt and pepper in shallow bowl or baking dish until well blended.
2. Place four bread slices on work surface. Top with basil, sun-dried tomatoes, cheese and remaining bread slices.
3. Heat oil in large nonstick skillet over medium heat. Dip sandwiches in egg mixture, turning and pressing to coat completely. Add sandwiches to skillet; cook 5 minutes per side or until golden brown. Cut into halves or strips.

RED ONION AND PARMESAN FOCACCIA

MAKES 12 SERVINGS

- **1¼ cups warm water (105° to 115°F), divided**
- **3 tablespoons honey, divided**
- **1 package (¼ ounce) active dry yeast**
- **3½ cups all-purpose flour**
- **¼ cup cornmeal**
- **8 tablespoons extra virgin olive oil, divided**
- **3 teaspoons salt, divided**
- **¼ cup balsamic vinegar**
- **¼ cup red wine vinegar**
- **½ red onion, thinly sliced into rings or slices**
- **½ cup grated Parmesan cheese**
- **Black pepper**

1. Combine ¼ cup water, 2 tablespoons honey and yeast in large bowl of stand mixer; stir to dissolve yeast. Let stand 5 minutes or until bubbly. Add flour, cornmeal, 3 tablespoons oil, 2 teaspoons salt and remaining water; stir to form dough. Attach dough hook to mixer; knead at low speed 5 minutes or until dough is smooth and elastic. Place dough in large greased bowl; turn to grease top. Cover and let rise in warm place 1 hour or until doubled in size.

2. Meanwhile, whisk vinegars, remaining 1 tablespoon honey and remaining 1 teaspoon salt in medium bowl. Add onion; stir until blended. Cover and marinate at room temperature.

3. Place 3 tablespoons oil in deep 9-inch round baking pan or springform pan (wrap bottom and side of springform pan with foil to prevent oil drips). Turn out dough into pan; press dough to fill pan. Dimple dough all over with fingers. Cover and let rise in warm place 30 minutes or until doubled in size.

4. Preheat oven to 400°F. Sprinkle half of cheese over dough; drain onions and arrange over cheese. Sprinkle with remaining cheese and drizzle with remaining 2 tablespoons oil. Sprinkle with pepper.

5. Bake 25 to 30 minutes until top is firm and golden brown. Cool slightly in pan; remove from pan to cutting board. Cut into wedges to serve. Serve warm.

NIÇOISE PIZZA

MAKES 4 SERVINGS

- 4 ounces goat cheese
- ½ cup ricotta cheese
- ½ cup minced fresh basil
- 1 teaspoon black pepper
- 1 (12-inch) prepared pizza crust
- 2 tablespoons extra virgin olive oil, divided
- 1 large red onion, cut in half and sliced
- ¼ pound fresh green beans, trimmed and cut into pieces
- 1 yellow or red bell pepper, seeded and cut into thin strips
- 3 tablespoons sliced black olives
- ½ cup shredded Parmesan cheese

1. Preheat oven to 450°F. Combine goat cheese, ricotta cheese, basil and black pepper until blended. Spread on pizza crust to within ½ inch of edge.

2. Heat 1 tablespoon oil in large skillet over medium heat. Add onion; cook and stir 8 to 10 minutes or until onion is very tender and brown. Arrange on top of cheese mixture.

3. Heat remaining 1 tablespoon olive oil in same skillet over medium heat. Add beans; cook and stir 1 minute. Add bell pepper; cook and stir 5 minutes or until crisp-tender. Arrange on top of onion. Top with olives; sprinkle with Parmesan cheese.

4. Bake 8 to 10 minutes or until cheeses are softened and crust is lightly browned.

GREEK SPINACH CHEESE ROLLS

MAKES 15 ROLLS

- **1 loaf (1 pound) frozen bread dough, thawed according to package directions**
- **1 package (10 ounces) frozen chopped spinach, thawed and squeezed dry**
- **¾ cup (3 ounces) crumbled feta cheese**
- **½ cup (2 ounces) shredded Monterey Jack cheese**
- **4 green onions, thinly sliced**
- **1 teaspoon dried dill weed**
- **½ teaspoon garlic powder**
- **½ teaspoon black pepper**

1. Spray 15 standard (2½-inch) muffin cups with nonstick cooking spray. Roll out dough into 15×9-inch rectangle on lightly floured surface. (If dough is springy and difficult to roll, cover with plastic wrap and let rest 5 minutes.)

2. Combine spinach, feta cheese, Monterey Jack cheese, green onions, dill, garlic powder and pepper in large bowl; mix well. Spread spinach mixture evenly over dough, leaving 1-inch border on long sides.

3. Starting with long side, roll up tightly; pinch seam to seal. Place roll seam side down; cut crosswise into 15 slices with serrated knife. Place slices cut sides up in prepared muffin cups. Cover with plastic wrap; let stand in warm place 30 minutes or until dough is slightly puffy. Preheat oven to 375°F.

4. Bake 20 to 25 minutes or until golden brown. Serve warm or at room temperature. Store leftovers in airtight container in refrigerator up to 2 days.

SWEETS

BLACKBERRY PANNA COTTA

MAKES 6 SERVINGS

- 3 cups frozen blackberries, thawed
- 2 cups whipping cream
- 1 cup buttermilk
- ¾ cup sugar
- 3 tablespoons water
- 1 package (¼ ounce) unflavored gelatin

1. Process blackberries in food processor or blender until smooth. Combine cream, buttermilk and sugar in medium saucepan; cook and stir over medium heat until sugar dissolves. Add blackberry purée; bring to a simmer over low heat.

2. Pour water into small saucepan. Sprinkle with gelatin; heat over low heat, swirling pan until gelatin is dissolved. Add to blackberry mixture; stir until blended.

3. Strain mixture through fine mesh sieve or strainer, pressing down with rubber spatula. Pour evenly into six 8-ounce ramekins or custard cups; refrigerate 6 hours or until set. To serve, invert and unmold onto serving plates.

BAKLAVA

MAKES ABOUT 32 PIECES

- 4 cups walnuts, shelled pistachio nuts and/or slivered almonds (1 pound)
- 1¼ cups sugar, divided
- 2 teaspoons ground cinnamon
- ¼ teaspoon ground cloves
- 1 cup (2 sticks) butter, melted
- 1 package (16 ounces) frozen phyllo dough (about 20 sheets), thawed
- 1½ cups water
- ¾ cup honey
- 2 (2-inch-long) strips lemon peel
- 1 tablespoon fresh lemon juice
- 1 cinnamon stick
- 3 whole cloves

1. Place half of walnuts in food processor. Pulse until nuts are finely chopped, but not pasty. Transfer to large bowl; repeat with remaining nuts. Add ½ cup sugar, ground cinnamon and ground cloves to nuts; mix well.

2. Preheat oven to 325°F. Brush 13×9-inch baking dish with some of melted butter or line with foil, leaving overhang on two sides for easy removal. Unroll phyllo dough and place on large sheet of waxed paper. Trim phyllo sheets to 13×9 inches. Cover phyllo with plastic wrap and damp, clean kitchen towel to prevent drying out.

3. Place one phyllo sheet in bottom of dish, folding in edges to fit; brush with butter. Repeat with seven additional phyllo sheets, brushing each sheet with butter as it is layered. Sprinkle about ½ cup nut mixture evenly over layered phyllo. Top nuts with three additional layers of phyllo, brushing each sheet with butter. Sprinkle with ½ cup nut mixture. Repeat layering and brushing of three phyllo sheets with ½ cup nut mixture two more times. Top final layer of nut mixture with remaining phyllo sheets, brushing each sheet with butter.

4. Score baklava lengthwise into four equal sections, then cut diagonally at 1½-inch intervals to form diamond shapes. Sprinkle top lightly with water to prevent top phyllo layers from curling up during baking. Bake 50 to 60 minutes or until golden brown.

5. Meanwhile, combine 1½ cups water, remaining ¾ cup sugar, honey, lemon peel, lemon juice, cinnamon stick and whole cloves in

medium saucepan; bring to a boil over high heat. Reduce heat to low; simmer 15 minutes. Strain hot syrup; drizzle evenly over hot baklava. Cool completely in baking dish on wire rack. Cut into pieces along score lines.

CITRUS OLIVE OIL CAKE

MAKES 10 SERVINGS

- 2 cups all-purpose flour
- 1 teaspoon salt
- 1 teaspoon baking powder
- ½ teaspoon baking soda
- 1½ cups sugar
- Grated peel and juice of 2 lemons
- 3 eggs
- 1 cup extra virgin olive oil
- ¾ cup milk

CANDIED LEMON PEEL (OPTIONAL)

- ½ cup granulated sugar
- ½ cup water
- 2 lemons, thinly sliced

1. Preheat oven to 350°F. Grease and flour deep 9-inch round baking pan or springform pan (wrap bottom and side of springform pan with foil to catch drips). Line bottom of pan with parchment paper. Whisk flour, salt, baking powder and baking soda in medium bowl.

2. Combine 1½ cups sugar and lemon peel in large bowl. Mix with electric mixer at low speed 2 minutes or until well blended and fragrant. Add eggs; beat at medium speed 3 minutes (mixture will be pale and fluffy). With mixer running on medium-low speed, add oil in thin steady stream. Stop and scrape bowl.

3. Place lemon juice in 2-cup liquid measuring cup. Add milk to equal 1 cup. With mixer running on low speed, add milk mixture alternately with flour mixture, beating just until blended after each addition. Pour batter into prepared pan; smooth top. Bang pan on counter once to remove air bubbles.

4. Bake 50 to 55 minutes or until top is dark golden, center is no longer jiggly and toothpick inserted into center comes out clean. Cool completely in pan on wire rack. Run thin knife around edge of cake; remove side of springform pan or invert onto plate.

5. Meanwhile for candied lemon, if desired, combine ½ cup sugar, ½ cup water and sliced lemons in small saucepan; cook over medium-low heat 20 to 30 minutes or until lemons are softened and translucent. Arrange lemon slices over top of cake; drizzle with some of syrup from saucepan, if desired.

ITALIAN ICE

MAKES 4 SERVINGS

- 1 cup sugar
- 1 cup sweet or dry fruity white wine
- 1 cup water
- 1 cup fresh lemon juice
- 2 egg whites*
- Fresh berries (optional)

***Use only grade A clean, uncracked eggs, preferably pasteurized.**

1 Combine sugar, wine and water in small saucepan. Cook over medium-high heat until sugar is dissolved and syrup boils, stirring frequently. Cover; boil 1 minute. Uncover; adjust heat to maintain simmer. Simmer 10 minutes without stirring. Remove from heat. Refrigerate 1 hour or until syrup is completely cool.

2 Stir lemon juice into cooled syrup. Pour into 9-inch round baking pan. Freeze 1 hour.

3 Quickly stir mixture with fork to break up ice crystals. Freeze 1 hour more or until firm but not solid. Meanwhile, place medium bowl in freezer to chill.

4 Beat egg whites in small bowl with electric mixer at high speed until stiff peaks form. Remove lemon mixture from pan to chilled bowl. Immediately beat lemon mixture with whisk or fork until smooth. Fold in egg whites. Spread mixture evenly into same baking pan. Freeze 30 minutes. Stir with fork; cover pan with foil. Freeze at least 3 hours or until firm.

5 To serve, scoop ice into dessert dishes. Garnish with berries.

PLUM-GINGER BRUSCHETTA

MAKES 9 SERVINGS

- **1 sheet frozen puff pastry (half of 17¼-ounce package)**
- **2 cups chopped, unpeeled, firm ripe plums (about 3 medium)**
- **2 tablespoons sugar**
- **2 tablespoons chopped candied ginger**
- **1 tablespoon all-purpose flour**
- **2 teaspoons fresh lemon juice**
- **⅛ teaspoon ground cinnamon**
- **2 tablespoons apple jelly or apricot preserves**

1. Unfold puff pastry and thaw 30 minutes on lightly floured work surface. Preheat oven to 400°F. Line baking sheet with parchment paper.

2. Cut puff pastry sheet lengthwise into three strips. Cut each strip crosswise in thirds to make nine pieces. Place on prepared baking sheet. Bake 10 minutes or until puffed and lightly browned.

3. Meanwhile, combine plums, sugar, ginger, flour, lemon juice and cinnamon in medium bowl.

4. Gently brush each piece of pastry with about ½ teaspoon jelly; top with scant ¼ cup plum mixture. Bake about 12 minutes or until fruit is tender.

CAFFÈ EN FORCHETTA

MAKES 6 SERVINGS

- 1 cup milk
- 1 cup whipping cream
- 4 eggs
- ½ cup sugar
- 2 tablespoons instant coffee or espresso
- Grated orange peel or chocolate-covered coffee beans (optional)

1. Preheat oven to 325°F.
2. Whisk milk, cream, eggs, sugar and coffee in large bowl until coffee is dissolved and mixture is foamy. Pour into 6 individual custard cups. Place cups in 13×9-inch baking pan. Fill pan with hot water halfway up sides of cups.
3. Bake 55 to 60 minutes or until knife inserted halfway between center and edge comes out clean. Serve warm or at room temperature. Garnish with grated orange peel, if desired.

NOTE

Enjoy your after-dinner coffee a whole new way. Translated from Italian, Caffè en Forchetta literally means "coffee on a fork."

INDEX

METRIC CONVERSION CHART

VOLUME MEASUREMENTS (dry)

1/8 teaspoon = 0.5 mL
1/4 teaspoon = 1 mL
1/2 teaspoon = 2 mL
3/4 teaspoon = 4 mL
1 teaspoon = 5 mL
1 tablespoon = 15 mL
2 tablespoons = 30 mL
1/4 cup = 60 mL
1/3 cup = 75 mL
1/2 cup = 125 mL
2/3 cup = 150 mL
3/4 cup = 175 mL
1 cup = 250 mL
2 cups = 1 pint = 500 mL
3 cups = 750 mL
4 cups = 1 quart = 1 L

VOLUME MEASUREMENTS (fluid)

1 fluid ounce (2 tablespoons) = 30 mL
4 fluid ounces (1/2 cup) = 125 mL
8 fluid ounces (1 cup) = 250 mL
12 fluid ounces (1 1/2 cups) = 375 mL
16 fluid ounces (2 cups) = 500 mL

WEIGHTS (mass)

1/2 ounce = 15 g
1 ounce = 30 g
3 ounces = 90 g
4 ounces = 120 g
8 ounces = 225 g
10 ounces = 285 g
12 ounces = 360 g
16 ounces = 1 pound = 450 g

DIMENSIONS

1/16 inch = 2 mm
1/8 inch = 3 mm
1/4 inch = 6 mm
1/2 inch = 1.5 cm
3/4 inch = 2 cm
1 inch = 2.5 cm

OVEN TEMPERATURES

250°F = 120°C
275°F = 140°C
300°F = 150°C
325°F = 160°C
350°F = 180°C
375°F = 190°C
400°F = 200°C
425°F = 220°C
450°F = 230°C

BAKING PAN SIZES

Utensil	Size in Inches/Quarts	Metric Volume	Size in Centimeters
Baking or Cake Pan (square or rectangular)	8×8×2	2 L	20×20×5
	9×9×2	2.5 L	23×23×5
	12×8×2	3 L	30×20×5
	13×9×2	3.5 L	33×23×5
Loaf Pan	8×4×3	1.5 L	20×10×7
	9×5×3	2 L	23×13×7
Round Layer Cake Pan	8×1½	1.2 L	20×4
	9×1½	1.5 L	23×4
Pie Plate	8×1¼	750 mL	20×3
	9×1¼	1 L	23×3
Baking Dish or Casserole	1 quart	1 L	—
	1½ quart	1.5 L	—
	2 quart	2 L	—